FOOD TRUCK BUSINESS

BRIAN PRICE

© Copyright 2020 by - All rights reserved. This document is geared towards providing exact and reliable information in regards to the topic and issue covered. The publication is sold with the idea that the publisher is not required to render accounting, officially permitted, or otherwise, qualified services. If advice is necessary, legal or professional, a practiced individual in the profession should be ordered. - From a Declaration of Principles which was accepted and approved equally by a Committee of the American Bar Association and a Committee of Publishers and Associations. In no way is it legal to reproduce, duplicate, or transmit any part of this document in either electronic means or in printed format. Recording of this publication is strictly prohibited and any storage of this document is not allowed unless with written permission from the publisher. All rights reserved. The information provided herein is stated to be truthful and consistent, in that any liability, in terms of inattention or otherwise, by any usage or abuse of any policies, processes, or directions contained within is the *solitary and utter responsibility of the recipient reader. Under no circumstances will any legal responsibility or blame be held against the publisher for any reparation, damages, or monetary loss due to the information herein, either directly or indirectly. Respective authors own all copyrights not held by the publisher. The information herein is offered for informational purposes solely and is universal as so. The presentation of the information is without contract or any type of guarantee assurance. The trademarks that are used are without any consent, and the publication of the trademark is without permission or backing by the trademark owner. All trademarks and brands within this book are for clarifying purposes only and are owned by the owners themselves, not affiliated with this document.*

Disclaimer

Disclaimer and Terms of Use: The Author and Publisher has strived to be as accurate and complete as possible in the creation of this book, notwithstanding the fact that he does not warrant or represent at any time that the contents within are accurate due to the rapidly changing nature of the Internet. While all attempts have been made to verify information provided in this publication, the Author and Publisher assume no responsibility for errors, omissions, or contrary interpretation of the subject matter herein. Any perceived slights of specific persons, peoples, or organizations are unintentional. In practical advice books, like anything else in life, there are no guarantees of results. Readers are cautioned to rely on their own judgment about their individual circumstances and act accordingly. This book is not intended for use as a source of legal, medical, business, accounting or financial advice. All readers are advised to seek services of competent professionals in the legal, medical, business, accounting, and finance fields.

TABLE OF CONTENT

Chapter 1: Introduction

Chapter 2: Breaking Into The Food Truck Industry

    2.1: A Big Mistake To Avoid When Starting Your Own Mobile Food Truck

Chapter 3: How To Start A Food Truck Business A-Z

    3.1: Starting A Food Truck

Chapter 4: Factors To Consider When Starting A Food Truck Business

Chapter 5: Starting A Profitable Food Truck Business

5.1: Learn How To Get Customers Buying From Your Food Truck

5.2: Building A Food Truck To Be Profitable At Minimum Cost

Chapter 6: Successful Food Truck Marketing

6.1: Marketing – 5 Lessons I Learned From Food Trucks

Chapter 7: Importance Of Social Media To Food Truck Business

Chapter 8: Benefits Of Starting A Food Truck Venture

Chapter 9: How To Get Customers To Your Food Truck

9.1: Qualities That A Food Truck Vendor Must Have

9.1: Tips On Planning A Menu For Your Food Truck

Chapter 10: Reasons Why Food Trucks Are Hot Right Now

Chapter 11: The Anatomy Of Food Trucks – Fast Food Just Got Faster

11.1: Food Trucks Vs Restaurants On The Environment

11.2: Maintaining Your Food Truck In The Winter

Chapter 12: Incorporating Food Trucks Into Private Party Catering

12.1: Specialized Insurance For The Food Street Vendor And Food Truck

Chapter 13: Reasons Why Your Business Or Charity Should Partner With A Food Truck

Chapter 14: Food Trucks – An Ideal Alternative To Restaurants

14.1: Wedding Menu Trend – Food Trucks

14.2: How To Sell Out Your Entire Food Truck In 45 Minutes

Chapter 15: Adjusting Your Food Truck's Menu To Entice More Customers

Chapter 16: Easy Steps To Build A Great Food Truck

Chapter 17: How The Trucking Industry Is Adapting To The Sustainable Food Trend

17.1: Food Services On A Vehicle

Chapter 18: Conclusion

Chapter 1: INTRODUCTION

Food trucks have been around for a long time. They're intended to take into account the requirements of individuals who don't have a lot of time during their mid-day break. Most vending trucks are found close to workplaces and offices. When contrasted with cafés and restaurants, food trucks have proven to be productive. If you can guarantee hungry clients that the food you are going to serve them is delicious and healthy then you will be extremely fruitful in the food truck business.

- The most significant component of a vending truck business is simply the vehicle. You have a ton of alternatives as there are a lot of varieties of vehicles that you can transform into a food truck, however, is picking the right vehicle for your business you should pick one that will best suit your business and its temperament.

After you have picked the right vehicle that you can transform into a vending truck, the following thing that you have to put resources into is the equipments that you will need for the operation of your food truck. Ovens, grills, refrigerators, and stainless steel are the couple of things that you ought to organize. You can likewise include different embellishments, for example, cutlery sets, condiments containers, racks, and plates.

In order for you to be able to maintain your business easily, there are a few guidelines that you have to follow. The main thing that you ought to do is to secure a permit for mobile food service. The mobile food service permit will fill in as an assurance to your clients that your truck has been examined by your local government specialists and that there are no issues identifying with the cleanliness or sanitation of your food truck or the food you're offering to the general public.

- If you want to have a food truck business yet your funds hinder you from purchasing a vehicle and required equipments, there are a ton of franchise organizations that can support you. You can purchase their items at a lower cost. These franchise organizations will likewise give all of you the gear/equipment that you need in setting up the business.

Owning a food truck business has a huge amount of upsides. You can go to various areas at one day and you are certain that your business won't go down simply like different organizations do. This is on the grounds that you are serving one of the basic products in life and you can serve them in better places. Regardless of where you go, there will constantly be hungry clients searching for cheap yet healthy and delicious food.

When you can purchase a food truck, this implies you are prepared to begin a business. Anyway, a food truck business isn't always a luxurious situation. You can expect the best results from having this business yet you should likewise envision the most noticeably awful. The most exceedingly terrible being, the potential outcomes of the truck stalling in your course. If this happens you will lose a great deal of cash and will leave hungry clients. In this business, you should have the option to locate a generally excellent and effective truck and you should keep up its great condition.

Here is a rule that you can take in the event that you need to purchase a food truck:

Recognize the sum that you are happy to spend on your business. When you have made a rough estimate on the amount you are willing to spend devise a business methodology and an arrangement that you think will work best for you. You should likewise be sure about your choice on what kind of truck you will utilize. Pick whether you need to contribute on a pre-owned truck or a fresh out of the plastic new truck.

Know the significance of asking the food vending business fundamentals from individuals who used to own food trucks. Ask them where they purchased their trucks and ask them which organizations are the most dependable. Knowing these in arrangement will assist you with sparing a ton of time and cash.

If you settle on purchasing a pre-owned truck, it is significant for you to have a specialist that you can bring along when you might want to assess the truck. There might be defects that can't be controlled by a layman's eye and that lone a specialist can disentangle. The specialist can assist you with looking at whether the pre-owned truck you wish to purchase is still in acceptable condition. If you can't bring a specialist along, request that the vendor give you an opportunity to have the food truck you plan to purchase be inspected by a mechanic. Bring the food truck to a mechanic and have the food truck exposed to a general review before choosing to purchase the unit.

Then again, if you feel that it would be a more wise and an increasingly handy choice to purchase another truck, ensure that the truck you purchase is warrantied and discover the extent and the inclusion of the warranty that accompanies the truck. Ask all the fundamental inquiries that you have to ask before paying for the unit.

Take the food truck for a test drive. This will tell you to decide if you can easily move the truck. Ensure that every one of the pieces of the truck and you can easily observe the back view from its mirrors. This is a safety precautionary measure for you. If you imagine that the truck is different to move, request an alternate unit. You should observe that despite the fact that the truck is in acceptable condition, if it is something that is hard to move, then it isn't useful for your business.

When you have chosen which truck to purchase, approach your merchant for a decent arrangement on the cost. Most venders would cut the truck's unique value 20% less. Take advantage of this. Get familiar with the specialty of wheeling and dealing, but don't deal excessively. Just like you, these food truck merchants are also in the business and need to benefit.

Chapter 2: BREAKING INTO THE FOOD TRUCK INDUSTRY

In the present economy, like never before, individuals are searching for alternative sources of work for themselves. Toss a scramble of American business in with the general mish-mash, and you will locate that one of the biggest developing search areas on Internet locales, for example, Yahoo Search, Google, and Bing! is the Mobile Food Industry. Mobile Cuisine Magazine might want to support these potential merchants and the food truck industry by giving a progression of articles that will help every person in choosing if being a mobile food seller is the right vocation move for them.

Setting up your Menu

Number one, what on the planet would you say you are going to sell? There are an immense number of variables you have to take a look at before you settle on your choice. Where are you situated? What would you be able to cook? What do the individuals in your general vicinity believe merits spending their well-deserved cash on to feed themselves? Similarly, as any café proprietor must conclude, you should discover what suits you and your clients. Do you have a gourmet or expert culinary foundation? Possibly taking a simple thought like tacos, or barbeque, and giving them another turn on old recipes will excite the crowd.

When you have figured out what you will sell, you should make time and effort to consummate your recipes and procedure. Have loved ones assist you with taste tests. If you have enough investment capital, discover a promoting firm to run the tests for you. Discover what individuals like, and don't care for, and tailor your menu to the outcomes you get. One of the most noticeably terrible things a seller can do is starting prematurely and sells its client's bad food. Verbal exchange as publicizing works both ways. Sure it tends to be a positive, however, if you are serving poor tasting food, it very well may be practically difficult to turn that perception around without having to rebrand your whole venture.

Location, Location, Location

Okay, you have it, you understand what you can and will be able to sell from your truck. Now what? All things considered, you have an item at the top of the priority list, yet whom and where will you sell it? Take a look at what kind of demographics will be keen on your food. It is safe to say that you are selling something that the late-night bar hoppers r will be keen on, or will you have to discover areas where the clients will have more enthusiasm for a gourmet food item, than fries and a hot dog? Travel around your zone. Locate the nearby joints; find where most of the urban areas pedestrian activity happens. If your rivals will be physical eateries, where are they found?

Since you have accumulated this information, you should discover where you will stop your rig. Numerous municipalities across the country over have severe rules on where mobile food sellers can stop. Take time and effort to talk with the zoning and parking authorities in the territories you wish to sell. Find out to what extent you can remain in one spot, find out the hours you can stop with or without feeding a meter. Another avenue food trucks are utilizing, is leaving in open lots. Contact the proprietors of the lots, and get their consent to stop there, and be certain the authorization is recorded as a hard copy.

You may need to supply them with times and days of the week you intend to utilize their lot. Instead of denying their solicitation and risk the loss chance to partner on their site, review a proposition with the necessary data which the two parties can consent to. Much of the time a level charge or a level of your deals might be essential to settling on an agreement; be that as it may, having a normal site for deals can be an incredible beginning to getting your business noticed.

Using your Competition

In most high traffic food truck communities it will be hard to fire up a business that will be unique. When you have figured out what kind of fare you will serve your clients, you should discover who your immediate culmination will be. Search the streets, the web and all the more critically, use twitter to track them down. Discover when they work and what their menu comprises of. Make certain to discover them and visit their locales. Other than attempting to discover what their clients are purchasing, the more significant part of your furtive endeavors ought to be to taste their product. If it's conceivable, return on various events, this methodology will give you a superior comprehension of how they work and how you can control your menu, your costs and your locations.

A BIG MISTAKE TO AVOID WHEN STARTING YOUR OWN MOBILE FOOD TRUCK

A few days ago I was counseling a customer wanting to open his very own food truck. Superficially he seemed like he had truly considered this and even had secured some sponsorship.

He was prepared to "move" full steam ahead. My first inquiry was to ask him about his idea. Well, it took him around 45 minutes to disclose everything to me and I am as yet not certain I understand it completely.

HIS BIG MISTAKE

He was from a foreign country and the food he offered me to taste was totally delectable. I don't know what it is called so I won't butcher the name here however trust me-once individuals tasted it they would adore it.

However, that was likewise his big mistake. He would need to prepare individuals to eat what he was serving. He would need to clarify how everything came about. He would need to explain the entirety of the ingredients.

By the way - a portion of the ingredients are extremely elusive since they are from his local nation and not effectively available here. That obviously is BIG PROBLEM # 2.

If you will be successful with your own versatile food truck (café) your food must be effectively and immediately comprehended.

EVERYBODY UNDERSTANDS HAMBURGERS - TACOS-BURRITOS-PIZZA and obviously crepes and grill just to give some examples. Be that as it may, nobody would have comprehended his dishes. Without a doubt, people wouldn't have the option to articulate it by and large.

You likewise should have the option to get to your ingredients rapidly and reasonably. Ideally, you will come up short on food and you need to have the option to have an adequate stock of whatever you offer close by so you can restock rapidly.

Envision if for reasons unknown he couldn't locate these unique ingredients. He might be out of business.

Main concern: Make sure your idea is now acknowledged. Ensure you can rapidly and effectively (and modestly) have an abundant stock of ingredients close by constantly.

FOOD TRUCKS

Food trucks are a culinary phenomenon that have been clearing the nation in the course of the recent years. Similarly, as they have picked up fame all through the continental U.S, food trucks have gotten a staple in

Hawaii. Filling in as easygoing eateries, these mobile cafés are an incredible method to appreciate genuine island flavors without using every single cent.

During your stay in Oahu, attempt to find a balance between the meandering fare of food trucks and the upscale waterfront cafés so you can experience all parts of astounding Hawaiian cooking and the exquisite impacts of Hawaii's Asian neighbors. Food trucks are a particularly extraordinary lunchtime alternative, and they are commonly parked in focal areas. The absolute best to sample from include:

1. **Haili's Hawaiian Foods:** Haili's Hawaiian Foods is a nearby Hawaiian food truck that originally got its start as a catering food business for Oahu luaus. Situated under a hala tree close to Ward Theater, this truck is open during lunch hours on weekdays. Highlight dishes include pork and chicken laulau, lomi salmon, and other seafood dishes.

2. Elena's Restaurant: Elena's Restaurant incorporates a range of dishes propelled by Head Chef Elena's Filipino heritage. Elena's location pivots among key goals, including the air terminal, Waipio, and Ko Olina, and exact subtleties are accessible on the site. Some favorite dishes incorporate the pork adobo fried rice omelet and sari-sari.

3. Opal Thai: Opal Thai, initially a mobile food truck, is presently a casual, independent eatery. Notwithstanding, it gives an uncommon experience as each dish is customized by the cook as indicated by your very own food tastes and preferences. Its low key atmosphere has managed to save the food truck environment.

4. Leonard's Malasadas: The Portuguese motivated flavors of Leonard's malasadas will make your mouth water. Initially established as a bread shop, Leonard took his business to the streets with a white and red Malasadamobile. Typically, the truck can be

found in the Waikele Center in Waipahu throughout the day on the weekends.

5   Jawaiian Irie Jerk: Jawaiian Irie Jerk includes an uncommon blend of flavors by bridging the taste gap between Hawaii and Jamaica. The basic menu highlights authentic dishes from the proprietor's Jamaican hometown. This truck can be found at the side of Kalakaua Avenue and Kapiolani Boulevard close to the Hawaii Convention Center from lunch through dinner hours on Mondays through Saturdays.

Regardless of your preferences and tastes, Oahu is home to a food truck or casual diner with the right flavors. In view of its multicultural heritage, the Hawaiian islands are home to food impacts from the Polynesian islands, numerous Asian nations, and even Europe and the Caribbean.

Is Joining a Food Truck Franchise Right for You?

Most new food truck proprietors stroll into this industry with an entrepreneurial spirit, stirred due to, and in spite of, the poor economy, and all the more especially, the loss of job. Given this downturn, and despite of it, we have seen a national ascent in the food truck industry. This industry has brought forth imaginative, diverse and delightful foods that are sweeping the country, one mile at a time.

When we think about the word 'entrepreneur,' we regularly overlook that this word doesn't just imply people that have made business thoughts from scratch. Rather, entrepreneurs are business owners that have taken on types of risk that the vast majority are reluctant or incapable to effectively manage.

This definition opens up an entire other course for aspiring food truck entrepreneurs to take on. Instead of making it necessary to suddenly become a brand-advertising expert, creative designer, or master chef, you may choose to turn into a food truck franchisee -

which accompanies the greater part of the advantages of working in the food truck industry with less of the duty. It's ideal for people who have next to zero business foundation.

But how can you conclude whether to be an entrepreneurial franchisee or go into business from scratch? Essentially, it comes down to the level of association you need in settling on choices for your operation.

How about we take a look at a rundown of the pros and cons of joining an franchise:

Pros:

- There are less forthcoming decisions. Within a franchise, you are given instant brand acknowledgment. The menu, the name, design are given to you.

- You'll have the expert help you need. The corporate office will provide you with help and staff that can address concerns and questions. This can be particularly useful for new business owners in the mobile food industry, as they may be new to how to manage issues that emerge.
- You have a name. What's more, with that name comes business. Your name is as of now known all through the city, state, and, now and sometimes, even the entire country.

Cons:

- Food truck franchisees need capital - and loads of it. These endeavors can run up to $500,000 just to join them. What's more, commonly, this price tag goes against the reason that business owners are looking to go into this industry in any case. All things considered, opening up a food truck should be a lot less expensive than running a physical café, right?

- The idea of the truck - name, design, and menu - is given to you. Similarly, as this fills in as a pro for joining a franchise, it can likewise be viewed as a con. It takes into consideration little innovativeness, which is the thing that most business visionaries thrive on.
- You're paying royalties and other fees (relentless). In addition to the fact that you have to pay for the rights to franchise, you are likewise expected to pay royalties,

So, what will you choose? Keep up a receptive outlook and settle on key choices that are in line with your desires and personality. Opening any food truck business - regardless of whether it's a franchise or a truck from scratch is a long haul choice that shouldn't be trifled with.

Chapter 3: HOW TO START A FOOD TRUCK BUSINESS-A-Z

Owning a food truck business can be one of the most enjoyable of all business on the planet. Consider it! Feeding hungry individuals delicious, crisply cooked, luscious suppers at costs you'd pay at the neighborhood greasy spoon. Be that as it may, before going into this business, you must do some arranging and thinking, to make figure out if you have what it takes to be successful. As with getting into any business, there are numerous components that should be considered. At the base of every one of these contemplations is the issue: "Are you are prepared to work for yourself?"

You'll be decisive, aggressive, and prepared to work your arrangement perseveringly before you can hope to make progress. There are more food trucks hitting the lanes regular and it must be your mission to claim your place among them and at last ascent over the competition.

First, discover who and where the competition is. Make a rundown of the considerable number of cooking styles that you discover there, and choose what you can serve that will be unique and welcomed in your commercial center. Everything from your truck design, logo, to your choice of cooking, everything about your business must be remarkable. Obviously, you'll must be health-conscious, organized, and eco-friendly.

Take a look at a typical say, regardless of whether this situation energizes you or scares you half to death, may determine if you're up to be a gourmet food truck operator/owner.

5:00 am: Rise and shine. In a couple of hours most of the world will be awake and every one of them hungry. You have to get ready to sustain them.

5:30 am Daily stock up at the supermarket for crisp ingredients (could have been done the prior night if you have a POS system).

6:00 am: Drive to your assigned prep-kitchen, where you will meet your staff, and start getting ready food for the truck. For instance: cutting vegetables, allotting the dish partitions, preparing your exceptional sauces, and so forth.

8:30 am till night (or at whatever point you make your $ objective): serve that tasty food of your truck.

10:00 pm: Clean up, and prepare for another pack buster day tomorrow.

You'll require food creativity, knowledge, marketing skills, media skills, except if you go with one of the franchise food truck organizations around. Search for 'food truck franchises'. Industriousness is the name of the game. You should be sharp when leading your exploration on beginning your very own food truck business as there are numerous guidelines relating to a food truck that contrast dependent on every city. Check with the interstate division of your local authority for its specific guidelines.

Trucks are mechanical so you'll need to arrange a reliable and responsive repairman. Concerning the apparatuses that accompany your truck, it is not smart thought to purchase used, you'll never know how the past proprietor cared for the truck. When new, these apparatuses are secured under their makers' guarantees. When you've purchased utilized, stovetop, a fridge, and oven will by necessity require maintenance.

With respect to the accounting, employing an accountant to deal with your business might be a bit expensive, so consider somebody who knows QuickBooks or some other accounting software program. A lawyer may be important to work out the permit and parking licenses, however here once more, there might be benefits out there that can help with this, at a fraction of the expense of a lawyer. Once more, make your search on Google.

Marketing? Yes, significant. I cannot overemphasize the significance of social media. Without it, your toast. No food truck has ever been effective without contacting people in general. The most prosperous food trucks use applications on mobile applications, Facebook and Twitter, among others. Keep in contact with clients, keeping them near you as much as could reasonably be expected is another key to an effective business. Furthermore, obviously, you need your client to know where you will be. Do a search on Food Truck mobile applications and see what's out there.

Not all food truck proprietors maintain their business full time. A few trucks work just on ends of the week or after work hours. Clearly, full-time activities, in the right area, will make more cash, yet on the other side, it requires duty. Whichever way you pick consistently keep a week by week schedule with set times for taking care of bills, paying taxes and obviously for spreading words of your business on the web and among peers.

After thinking and choosing a game-plan for your truck, write it down, make a business arrangement that will assist you with accomplishing your objectives quicker and all the more proficiently. What's more, a realistic business plan is basic in the event that you need to request loans from companions or the bank. Here as well, if you need loans, search online for Food Truck SBA loans. Everybody needs to see that their cash is heading off to a possibly lucrative venture, so the more intensive you are in setting up this business, the more effective you will be in persuading others to help.

So you're a food lover and you love to make unique delicious foods. You additionally love profiting and making people feel happy and fed. You are a business visionary on the most fundamental level and need to work for yourself, supporting a unique thought that you concocted. What's a better job than opening your own food business? A new generation of street food has made your job materialized. Why not begin a food truck business that will surely become a staple of the American culture and cheap food gourmet lifestyle?

The street food industry has never been this revived and rethought. Gifted gourmet experts and even self-starting food lovers may open up a mobile food truck for substantially less capital than opening up a café/restaurant while giving a similar quality food. Simple menus that concentrate on explicit cooking styles and even combinations of various sorts of food can be a moment hit. Fans will follow your locations through the web and by means of social media networking websites, for example, twitter, so your advertising expenses are practically free. As though that is insufficient incentive, simply a year ago there was a blasting 3 million food trucks in the U.S alone, which shows that it is a rewarding business, with significantly less investment risk.

The initial step is to choose which foods you enjoy making, are good at, and might want to share to the world. Consider foods that can be made in mass amounts, with sensible ingredients and will accommodate your financial limit. Not so complicated preparation is key because of the cooking condition inside food trucks. Your choice on which foods to sell ought to rely upon your experience at a business (keep it basic), the size of the business, the crowd you are taking into account, and your spending limit.

Demographic groups in your vicinity of service is essential since your potential client's needs will characterize the interest in your service (incredible food!) and your timetable of operation. You might need to choose which neighborhood will be your principle or common spots, and around what time (peak meal times) you might want to operate. In case you're feeling ambitious, perhaps think about lunchtime, supper time, and even late evening snacking time to work full force.

Consider your kick off expenses to ensure you remain within the spending plan. The field is so expansive and explicit to the kinds of food you need to sell that you truly must have everything listed out and analyzed. There's no formula, however, consider huge costs like the expense of the food truck, kitchen utilities, and supplies, initial food buys, licenses and enlistments, advertising, business insurance, and maintenance of your truck.

What's particularly exceptional about running a food truck business is that you should consider getting vehicle insurance and a comprehensive business insurance policy. Try not to stress, you're saving significantly already by cutting worker charges, rental expenses for a physical space and other expenses. Commercial vehicle insurance is needed in your industry since you will depend vigorously upon your truck every day. You wouldn't need it to break down, without having the best possible protection procedures to help spread the expenses of fixing.

HOW DO I START MY OWN FOOD TRUCK BUSINESS?

Are you are the kind of individual who knows there's a lot more out there than only an hourly job? Do you realize you could make it all alone in the event that you simply had a plan to follow? If this is the case, the food truck business could be the perfect decision for you.

Food truck concessions are intended to enable you to own your own business and serve top-notch food without having to deal with the high cost and hassle of owning an eatery. In any case, not all food truck business are of a similar quality.

At top mobile food franchises, you will get the experience of a demonstrated innovator in the quick casual food market. You begin with every one of the instruments you have to succeed including a solid business framework that you have access from the minute you consent to your Franchise Arrangement. What's more, these top franchises won't leave you out there all alone. You'll experience a broad training program system to enable you to succeed.

Never run a food concession? That is alright. Trusted franchises take you through the development and choice of your site, and help you directly through the Grand Opening and beyond. From stock control to prepare strategies, their proven systems wipes out the need to commit errors by trial and error. You're a success directly out of the entryway. What's more, when you succeed, they succeed. You're all in this together. These franchisees are fruitful in light of the fact that they set aside the effort to guarantee you're constantly supported from back-end office frameworks to everyday working inquiries.

Concerned about permit or hiring? Try not to be. The best mobile concessions will have frameworks set up for the work planning process just as full direction through permits and zoning. You'll appreciate electronic detailing and your very own food cost analysis framework so you can invest your energy serving your clients not managing heaps of paperwork.

Starting a food truck business is an energizing endeavor that doesn't require a huge money expense. You can search for low start-up expenses to guarantee you'll be experiencing your fantasy in as little as 90 days. You'll be offering your clients mobile food concessions unlike others. You can serve sought after foods like Vermont Farms Natural Chicken, grass-fed Vermont meat burgers, healthy vegetable wraps and top-quality frozen yogurt. The present day's top mobile food franchises are on the road to success to quick easygoing food success. The mobile food trailer business is getting a charge out of astounding development (14% and that's only the tip of the iceberg!) incredible in these hard economic times. You can be a part of that achievement.

STARTING A FOOD TRUCK

No, you can't be anything you desire although such a large number of us were told at a youthful age - If you can dream it you can accomplish it! Be that as it may, as we age we understand it's not true. Just a chosen few will turn into a well-known movie star, play in the NFL or become the President. Furthermore, as we age the vast majority of us understand that all we truly need is to live serenely, to be self-sufficient, to occasionally enjoy some of the better things in life and to be content with our loved ones.

Most of us are not millionaires nor billionaires and we don't need to be that in order to be happy. The vast majority of us would be excited making $7 to $10k every month. This sort of income is a long ways from millionaire status, however, it would enable us to live far over the larger part. It will allow for nice home clothes, cars, furniture, and vacations.

So how would you get there? What profession has the genuine potential to make that sort of salary and doesn't require a school or even a secondary school degree, it doesn't require excellent wellbeing, it doesn't require related knowledge and you can work for yourself?

Welcome to Street Food and beginning your very own food truck.

Anybody can do this effectively. Luck isn't required to be successful. You can begin with a hotdog truck, you can become familiar with the business and you can make somewhere in the range of $40k to $100k per year. There is no mystery menu or explicit aptitude required. You just need the right area, the right menu, and the right pricing. You'll accomplish the income and freedom that you need. It is possible and being done each and every day.

If you are inspired, at that point make the following steps. Peruse a few books, continue Googling, search YouTube and start plotting your path. As a youngster you likely didn't aspire to become a food trucker yet you're not a kid any longer and this is a great method to get from where you are today to where you need to be tomorrow.

Working for yourself will require a great deal of commitment and self-control. You need to make yourself to get off the sofa and go earn your living. Nobody is going to push you off your comfortable seat and cause you to do this. You will be the CEO and CFO of your organization. You will be responsible for each dime spent and earned. The buck stops at you. Ultimately a portion of these things can be assigned out, however, the entirety of this will require your management and responsibility for success. Like any job, there will be loads of difficult work

Cons of Food Trucking:

- This is work, it is difficult work and extended periods of time.
- Obtaining licenses
- Learning and following the city and state guidelines
- Obtaining insurance, license, and a commissary
- Inventory and prep work
- The daily tidy up
- Working around extraordinary climate or finding shielded zones

Pros of Food Trucking:

- Money! And loads of it. Regardless of whether you need two or three hundred dollars per week, several hundred a day or a couple hundred per hour... these are for the most part realistic figures in mobile concessions.
- Freedom! You make your very own hours. Work 1 day a week or work 7 days every week. Take a multi-week excursion at whatever point you need. It's up to you. You are the chief. This can also be perilous. So if you aren't spurred, this isn't for you. You'll wind up with a costly residue collector in your carport
- You can begin with next to zero cash
- No nagging boss's or corporate structure

So should you do this?

First, it tends to be financially rewarding and anybody can do this. There is a reason some NYC sellers will pay the city over $200k every year to work their Hot

Dog truck in a prime area. There is a reason there are more than two thousand mobile food sellers in NYC alone. There is serious cash to be made in this industry. Anywhere there is pedestrian activity there are profits.

This isn't an undertaking depending on a little luck for progress. The business just works! What's more, it works for everybody. Anybody placing in exertion and inspiration can secure an area that will benefit hundreds or thousands consistently.

If you are a culinary expert, business person, unemployed, wanting a supplemental salary, need a career change, resigned or simply exhausted and love to cook/serve peoples, at that point, this growing niche could be your purpose in life! This is perhaps the least demanding approach to go into business and start seeing genuine benefits from the very first moment.

Recollect this is work. You will require a permit, you should know state and city guidelines, taxes, licensing, insurance, inventory, a commissary, prep and the feared tidy up each day - you should do your exploration. Don't panic. This information is effectively possible and can be found with Google search.

So the one fundamental inquiry you're most likely posing - what sort of cash would I be able to make? And the appropriate response is - it just depends. What are you selling? What amount of pedestrian activity does your area get? How much do you intend to work?

If you are going full time, have great locations and if you are truly working hard you can expect at least $40k in your first year. As you become set up and grow more regulars your profits can drastically increase. There are merchants making six figures.

Chapter 4: FACTORS TO CONSIDER WHEN

STARTING A FOOD TRUCK BUSINESS

As of 2015, yearly incomes gotten from the food truck industry were over $1 billion. As per specialists, the industry is on a 9.3% development rate; along these lines, if you have for the longest time been wanting to venture into it, there has never been a better time than this to dive in. For you to begin a fruitful food truck business you have to place various elements into thought. These factors include:

Food concept

This is fundamentally a guide that will assist you with beginning effectively. For you to think of an idea you have to embrace a lot of research. You should explore the quick-moving food in your vicinity. You ought to likewise look into the gear that you require for the work. If you discover that coffee is fast-moving in your vicinity, one of the significant gear you have to have is extra room for water to mix coffee. Before you settle on your idea, undertake a trial and perceive how individuals react to it.

Legal entity

When conducting research on the food concept, also examine the best vehicle to purchase. There are numerous kinds of vehicles that you can purchase: You can utilize a van, you can use an SUV or a bus. Your vehicle choice ought to be informed by your region of activity, food that you will serve and your financial limit.

To give your business authenticity you have to enlist it with the significant legal bodies. Prerequisites fluctuate from one state to the next; in this way, you should contact the small business administration to get information on the licenses and permits that you require to be in operation.

In addition to giving your business a genuine look, enlisting your business additionally decreases your own obligation if an issue comes up with the truck. In addition to getting licenses and permits, also guarantee that you register your business with the inward internal revenue service (IRS) or some other relevant tax body.

Regardless of whether your business is little, it's constantly suggested that you retain a local accountant and lawyer. The experts prove to be useful in helping you handle the financial and legal parts of the business.

Insurance

Much the same as some other vehicle you have to get insurance for your food truck. While getting insurance recall that various organizations charge different charges; subsequently, you should research and find an affordable and reputable insurance provider. For peace of mind, make sure the policy you take covers the sensitive regions of the truck. These include Food supplies, truck, equipment, and any other thing.

Getting the word out

For you to make deals and manufacture a brand you have to advertise your business. Two of the most dominant channels that you can utilize are social media and words of the mouth. When you serve incredible foods and keep up great associations with your customers you will get the word out about your business. Utilize social media to announce offers and any report about the business. Social media platform that you should utilize are Facebook, Twitter, Instagram, Snapchat and so on.

Chapter 5: STARTING A PROFITABLE FOOD TRUCK BUSINESS

A food truck business can be very gainful as there are countless individuals who normally eat at mobile restaurants. Rather than waiting that clients to come to your business, you can go to where they are and draw them in with a special exhibit of delicious dishes.

You can begin and maintain a food truck business with considerably less staff than what you would require to run a standard eatery. It is also more affordable and includes lower overhead costs when contrasted with a customary eatery business.

You should start by having a reasonable arrangement for your business. You have to pick a definite specialty in the food business regarding the dishes served and the type of clients you wish to target. Since the greater aspects of your business would rely upon these components, you have to pick them at the very beginning. You have to know whether you need to sell fast food, ice cream, soups, pastries, or multi-cuisine food. You additionally need to realize the age range that you would target – whether teenagers, children, executives, college crowds, or senior citizens. Despite the fact that there would be an overlap in age groups, you need to have your target clients at the top of the priority list before kicking off your business.

You additionally need to have a particular objective at the top of the priority list for your business. What will your business be in the following five or ten years? How many more trucks and workers would you use at that point? What is the sort of income you are seeking in the future? These are some of the objectives that you have to set for your business at the very beginning.

When you include a reasonable picture inside you with respect to what you wish to do, at that point you can approach securing the proper permits and licenses for your business. You should also know that specific towns and urban areas that don't permit you to run a food truck business. So you have to pick your business area dependent on the laws in force in the district.

When you have the licenses, you have to procure a food truck for your business. You can buy a used or a new truck, or even lease or rent one for a specific timeframe. You may need to find a proper bank or a private investor in the event that you require subsidizing for your business.

When you have all these setup, you can start running your business right away. The key to being fruitful in the mobile food business is being special and offering something that nobody else offers. Individuals search for assortment and novelty constantly. If you can deliver what they need, you can turn out to be extremely successful in the Food Truck Business.

HOW DO I KNOW I'VE FOUND THE BEST FOOD TRUCK BUSINESS?

Not every person who offers a meal on the goal is in a similar class. To locate the right mobile food truck business you need to do some exploration. Do you need a concession business like the one on every other corner? Or would you like to be the food concession that offers a crisp and remarkable menu that stands in a class without anyone else's input?

You start a new business for yourself since you want profit. So as to do that, you need to pick your activity carefully. A decent mobile food truck framework will give all the essential resources, tools, and devices to make sure you get out of the gate rapidly and effectively. Giving this a shot on your own will positively prompt numerous stumbles and wrong turns. Do you believe you have the opportunity and cash to risk going alone? So before settling on anything, discover an industry leader who has a training program set up and frameworks intended to save you years of error and trial.

The best mobile food business has a proven plan of action that is fabricated and intended to draw in clients from a wide section of the population. They furnish you with training from the day you consent to your Franchise Agreement and backing for whatever length of time that you are ready to go.

Where lunch clients once needed to agree to tasteless burgers, frozen-flat, sandwiches, and frozen fries with barely any choices, the best mobile food concessions offered hand-tapped Vermont beef burgers and healthy decisions, for example, an assortment of new wraps. They have developed exponentially every year and keep on outperforming expectations even in a bleak economy. When you decide to collaborate with the top mobile concession franchises, you will be maintaining a mobile food business with heart. You and your staff will make some incredible memories serving clients with a full menu of fascinating and healthy choices. Also, when you're working in a confined space, there's no space for mistake. Your training gives all of you the plans and food readiness conventions that you have to pull in your demographic and surpass their expectations every single visit. What's more, their state of the art online detailing frameworks and back-office support mean you never need to manage long stretches of paperwork.

GETTING STARTED WITH A MOBILE FOOD TRUCK BUSINESS

Mobile cooking alludes to selling food out of some kind of mobile vehicle, either a van or truck in many events. It is like normal cooking since the food is brought legitimately to the clients, but is served directly out the vehicle instead of inside a structure. Mobile cooking is famous in numerous urban areas where it is convenient to get food on the run, and it is an incredible business opportunity for those hoping to get into the food business.

A mobile food truck is an incredible investment for anybody keen on getting into the food business since it doesn't expect one to purchase or rent a whole eatery/restaurant. Rather, people can sell their homemade goods directly out of a moving vehicle and can make a trip to a well-known location where they realize they can make enough profit.

An ice-cream van is like a mobile food truck since they were invented so as to convey ice cream to individuals strolling in the city. A mobile food truck or van is structured like an ice cream van since it has an enormous window that makes it simple to converse with clients. Within the van is totally extraordinary, however, since ice cream vans are full of freezers so as to keep the dessert cold. A mobile food truck is practically similar to a little and convenient kitchen since it contains a considerable lot of indistinguishable segments from a normal kitchen. It can contain spots to warm up food, a freezer and fridge and for storage, a sink for cleaning up, and even a beverage fountain for dispensing colas. They additionally contain areas for storage and even shelves for showing items, and a ledge for a cash register and storage for cups and dishes. They come in various varieties, and the buyer can choose which parts they need dependent on the menu they plan on selling.

Mobile kitchens can either be acquired as a mobile food van or truck or as a trailer that can snare straightforwardly onto the back of a vehicle. In any case, it makes it conceivable to move the food business to various areas, so as to discover well-known areas where individuals are probably going to be hungry. Although a mobile food truck proprietor may need to make a trip to a few areas when they first kick-off, they, for the most part, locate the most well-known areas and travel to them at the same time daily.

A mobile food truck or kitchen is an incredible buy for anybody getting into the food business, particularly since relatively few have the opportunity to sit in an eatery for a dinner any longer. It is a convenient method to sell food and appeal to a wide assortment of clients, and it doesn't require a tremendous initial investment like an eatery would. They typically just require a couple of individuals to operate and can pay for themselves in a matter of moments. A mobile food truck and kitchen is an incredible investment for anybody inspired by the food business, and can even change into a family partnership on the off chance that it increases enough fame.

LEARN HOW TO GET CUSTOMERS BUYING FROM YOUR FOOD TRUCK

Learn How To Get Client's Buying From Your Food Truck!

Breakfast 5:30-11:30 am Timing all you need.

In the event that your food truck will work during morning hours, offering a cooking intended for morning foods would clearly be important. Although expensive, a grinder ($1500) and coffee espresso system (over $3500) would be a delightful addition to the truck. In any case, would you say you are making a piece of art with your truck, or a business? Try not to lose sight who is going to your truck for his/her 'morning joe'. In the event that they needed a $4 double coffee, they'd almost certainly go to a cafe and sit down. Then again, don't ration the quality of coffee you use. You should offer a choice of crisply blended gentle to medium coffee, a solid mix, and a decaf mix (A decent machine should run about 500USD.).

Everything eggs is lovely, and if you need to get crepes, fancier, and waffles is an extraordinary expansion. Be that as it may, it would be ideal if you keep it basic to your benefit. Morning clients are by and large in a rush, so you can't take too long to even think about preparing.

Baked products from your preferred local baker are the ideal accessories to offer with your hot foods. Care ought to be taken with respect to who you buy these baked products. Here as well, don't get excessively detailed, clients need to eat and run.

The greater part of anything you need to serve hot for a morning meal fare can be set up on a blistering level top griddle. That leaves a lot of space for other hardware that can be utilized for prep of your lunch and supper cooking styles. "Little things create daily propensities," so by keeping your morning food basic, simple to-serve and modest, you can expect a one time fulfilled clients to stop by your truck the following day... And the next...

Lunch 11:30-5:30pm, Dinner 5:00-11:00pm

Now things get intriguing here. Hot dogs, pizzas, and hamburgers are available all over the place. It is preferable to be unique and creative in the design of your dinner and lunch fare. The dependable guideline doesn't change such a great amount from that of the morning cooking styles, which means, your client needs something quick, scrumptious and sensibly valued. Do a food that isn't found in the region in which you need to work. What's more, don't think about stopping too close to an existing café or restaurant! You'll make an adversary forever, also, the official or city authority may come down to you too. But, location is an alternate story, which I will write about at another point. In the event that your clients need to lounge around sitting tight for their order, they should sit serenely in an eatery. Keep your costs reasonable and ideally lower than neighborhood eateries with the goal that your food truck transforms into an increasingly wanted spot to go as well.

BUILDING A FOOD TRUCK TO BE PROFITABLE AT MINIMUM COST

When advising those wandering into the world with respect to mobile food truck business, I can't pressure enough the significance of building an "ideal" food truck. Furthermore, by ideal I don't mean the greatest, baddest, most costly new truck you can design only for the pure fun of it. You truly need to remember that you are building a food truck to yield maximum profits but at the very least cost, so you can look proficient and be fruitful, while keeping as much of those benefits as expected for yourself and your family! When you dig in, you will discover there can be a considerable amount to it. I truly need to give you a few mysteries directly here that I believe are the most significant contemplations, which ought to be sufficient to control you the right way.

Number one, I would unequivocally recommend you go with a quality utilized food truck. Furthermore, discovering one is in reality truly clear. A great deal of industrial trucks are already built to work for 300,000, 400,000, or even 500,000 miles! The sweet spot is regularly found by getting something like a FedEx or UPS truck, a bread delivery truck, or even a potato chip delivery truck. These models are genuine work horses and you could most likely discover one with around 100,000-120,000 miles at a not too bad cost; heck, even 150,000 miles still factors in a lot of useful worklife to begin and develop your mobile food business. What's more, guarantee the truck has been maintained, which undoubtedly it sure has been originating from FedEx,

UPS or any such enormous name truck fleet. You clearly need to get it checked at by a technician, however, this route will be your most affordable alternative and one that will work well for you in light of the fact that, once more, these things last 300,000, 400,000, 500,000 miles effectively.

When stocking your food truck, go for center of-the-line hardware that will be durable. What's more, I need to share with you here certain approaches to ensure yourself. I lost thousands of dollars because i didn't have the foggiest idea what to look for when I was enlisting the structure of my mobile kitchen. What's more, despite the fact that I did the research and went to five or six other truck manufacturers, regardless I got exploited. Building the truck is in some ways a bit like the Wild, Wild West. For reasons unknown there's not a great deal of regulation in this industry and I don't know why.

What I will urge you to do as far as ensuring you to do in terms of protecting yourself is to get a written contract and, when dealing with an out of state merchant, ensure that if there is a question that the agreement states it will be settled in your home state. Make that out-of-state merchant come to you if/with regards to it. The other thing I would do is make certain to pay them in thirds. By that I mean a third upon signing the agreement, a third midway through when you can expect the vehicle and ensure that it's tagging along on schedule, and afterward the last third once you've reviewed your food truck and it's delivered.

What's more, in further consideration when fabricating your food truck for maximum profit at minimum cost, ensure you go to your local jurisdiction and know their codes and laws first and afterward have your truck worked to those specs. Also, here's kind of a reward tip for you. Put in the contract that the truck must be built to these codes and specs and if they are not, the merchant will pay to have it adjusted. Try not to work this out after the build; do it in advance the right way while you have leverage with the manufacturer.

This is a serious mix-up I see numerous customers that I counsel with make. Sometimes it's too late by the time I get to them, but I need to ensure you don't commit this error. Ensure that you know the codes - and coincidentally, for each city or jurisdiction you're going to park in, you need to go to their health deartment and discover what their codes and laws are. Baltimore, happens to be one of the hardest in the country but yours can differ fiercely in certain perspectives.

Also, obviously, you need to ensure that your truck looks appealing. Recollect this is your mobile billboard and it creates catering jobs and new clients for your eatery. From individual experience, we really had the roof of a food truck taped, with the goal that when we went to a business district, the office business upper stories could see our site and a teaser message down there, so they could really order on the web and afterward come directly down to the truck and get their food.

To summarize everything, I would not prescribe going with low-end food truck gear nor would I propose going very good quality. The familiar saying of not being penny wise but pound foolish certainly applies to the mobile food industry. Pick carefully and save, however, don't purchase the least expensive hardware you can discover in the classifieds on the grounds that a breakdown is the exact opposite thing you need to be worrying about out there! I wish you achievement and bliss in your mobile food business attempts!

Chapter 6: SUCCESSFUL FOOD TRUCK MARKETING

How To Start a Successful Food Truck Marketing - Five Ways Of Attracting Attention!

1. Food truck occasions! A food truck occasion displays an extraordinary chance to attract the interest of both new and existing purchasers. These occasions are regularly composed by somebody attempting to make a buck on collecting rents to be a part of the occasion, but that is life in America. It very well may be justified, despite all the trouble, but you should verify who else will be there, and who is the clientele attending. You certainly don't need competition in your food. Furthermore, you would prefer not to serve your vegan cooking to a lot of rodeo types. In this way, similarly as with anything, thoroughly consider the cooperative energy of attending, and figure if the cost to do it merits the potential return.

Different sorts of occasions might be functions of associations that basically need to pull in individuals to their organization or events. These undertakings offer an enormous upside since you will be connected in the client's observation with the association supporting the occasion. That can give great PR.

A key factor to the accomplishment of an occasion relies upon the coordinator's investment into appropriate advertising of the occasion, to incorporate catchy posters and fliers. Some attention ought to be paid to you're food truck and the role it plays in the bigger event. Try not to be shy to demand what inclusion you and your truck will have in this advertising.

2. Putting resources into your very own Branding. Like your very own sauce as only one model. Here you will have the test of putting inadequate time and center to branding something that if you have no experience with it will be difficult. I propose you go with an organization that offers branding and marketing services. Branding has a gigantic upside, for it separates you from your opposition in a

memorable and unique way, its classy to have your own branded items.

3 Your name reveals everything... Or possibly it should try to. A name is generally critical to pass on in a short and direct a fashion as possible what you are, what you do, and in case of food, what you serve. What about Sizzle Stix (a Gourmet Street's brand) that sells tasty kabob foods skewered on a stick. Get it? What about Sweeties, they serve everything for the sweet tooth. What do you think the Dog Truck sells? (I'm not proposing this, you may get a young man who want to purchase a dog from you). But, you get my point, I hope. There's the "Take The Dump Truck." Can you think about what it sells? Dumplings... I don't think so!

4 Ensure your truck is appealing. It's genuinely counterproductive to spend all the cash on a new, completely equipped food truck, just to leave it standard and dull. A lovely vinyl wrap,

stupendously structured is definitely worth the cash and will attract in the eye of all who you drive by. Get innovative and make an external appearance that matches the alluring food you're offering inside.

5   Train your staff to have astounding customer service. It ought to be your #1 priority, as the initial five seconds of cooperation between another client and your staff will either make a client, or the inverse, best case scenario leave and a passer-by disinterested, and even under the least favorable conditions, cause somebody to insult your truck to other people. Train your staff to smile always, be selfless and benevolent.

MARKETING: 5 LESSONS I LEARNED FROM FOOD TRUCKS

Food Trucks have been springing up all over the nation. Everything scrumptiously sinful is on a truck. From cake shakes and fried Oreos to ginger Brussels grows and Short Rib Sandwiches...

When food truck lineups began, even better, one opened up directly before my Alma Mater, Johnson and Wales University. The BTTR (Biscayne Triangle Truck Round-up) Miami Food Truck Events, as a rule around 35 trucks, get together once per week.

My friends and I have been going for all intents and purposes each week, and the crowds continue getting bigger. From the start, it was mostly college students, and afterward individuals from all around the city started appearing.

And that made me wonder. "How did every one of these individuals find out about this?"

I chose to explore! I began watching the trucks, more significant asking questions. I thought of some amazing answers. This is what they do extraordinary, and what they could do:

1   They make a stand out brand personality.

The truck proprietors put a great deal of thought into thinking of an innovative name, and overall theme. The decals and truck configuration can make or break them. Some keep it basic and focus on making great food; others go insane with characters and graffiti-like structure. Just like in any business, standing out from your rivals is vital.

2   Most of them get the word out with Social Media.

Food Truck proprietors use Facebook and Twitter, since they move around a lot, so individuals can track them down. (Most of my friends find out about Food Trucks on Twitter or Facebook, and read reviews on which ones are ideal.)

3   About 75 percent of Food Trucks I saw have QR codes.

While individuals remain in line they ordinarily have their smart phones in their grasp. Food Truck proprietors ask that they scan the QR code to tail them on Facebook and Twitter, so they get the most recent updates.

4   Missed Opportunity?

I saw that a few trucks have 4" X 6" Flyers with QR Codes connected to Facebook, Twitter, their site and telephone number. For what reason aren't the proprietors approaching individuals to sign up for an email list? Missed chance? Why not gather their data and send them updates once per week about up and coming occasions.

5   Reviews!

Like most people, I have most loved Food Trucks. I'm fixated on this scrumptious, scrumdiddlyumptious (no genuine word can portray how great it is) Short Rib Sandwich. I talk about it on Facebook and my companions have all attempted it! Many individuals post reviews on Yelp or their own sites, so it's a smart thought to urge clients to review your business. A few trucks have a decal requesting that clients review them on Yelp.

FOOD TRUCKS: FROM FAD TO FIXTURE

America's most recent food fever truly isn't so new. Simply return to your childhood summers when the main thing that could separate ball games or pool parties other than a mother's voice was the sweet alarm call of the ice cream truck folding into your neighborhood.

Take that picture - aside from replace kids with business experts and change out the ice cream man for a gourmet culinary expert - and you have food trucks, coming to a city close you...if they haven't showed up already.

Experiencing childhood in Morocco, Yassir Raouli probably never heard an ice cream truck's melody. Be that as it may, in the wake of attempting numerous endeavors in New York City - waiting to tables, managing night clubs and opening an internet dress shop - Raouli thought of a thought, Bistro Truck, that could convey him to retirement.

"I did research, and I needed to begin an eatery. I always needed to have my very own place," he says. "What seemed well and good was the food truck."

If you still haven't caught on, the food truck is actually what it says it is. A whole café, from the kitchen to the cash register, is independent in a truck or van. Food truck proprietors, who regularly serve as the culinary specialists, drive their cafés to the people as opposed to letting the people come to them. From that point, you begin to see contrasts.

There are food trucks that cater just to the lunch crowd, and others to only the supper surge; some do both. Various food trucks are nomadic, posting a week's worth of areas on destinations, for example, Twitter and Facebook and making them dependent on their clients' Internet clever to direct them to their present areas. Others, similar to Raouli's activity, are parked day by day at the same spot in the same locality.

It's the accentuation set on the quality of food that characterizes the present wave of food trucks. Besides the venerable ice cream man, individuals have been eating road food in the United States for a considerable length of time - at hot dog trucks in Chicago or brat remains in Boston. Be that as it may, in the course of the most recent year's clients the nation over have had the pleasure of heap gastronomic alternatives. Los Angeles has a kosher taco truck (Takosher). Kronic

Krave Grill serves South American arepas four days every week in downtown Austin, Texas. What's more, of course, in Portland, Ore., proprietors pushed the politically right farthest point with Kim Jong Grillin', a Korean BBQ food truck named after the dubious North Korean dictator.

"I think we sort of revolutionized it," Raouli says of Bistro Truck's menu, whose day by day specials highlight things like chilled watermelon soup, kofta kebabs, and strawberry panna cotta. "We were one of the first to offer gourmet food."

Regardless of whether Raouli led the gourmet food truck revolution might be questionable, but the achievement of his Bistro Truck is certainly not. In late August 2010, on the one-year anni of its opening, Bistro Truck was named one of five finalists for New York City's yearly Vendy Awards, a food truck competition whose eccentric name gives a false representation of the aggressive reality of the occasion.

Bistro Truck's nomination should give the business some genuinely necessary reputation that can counterbalance the obstructions confronting food trucks. For instance, at customary eateries, any accident can be moderated by a treat or cocktail on the house. Food truck proprietors, however, are regularly restricted to a first impression. Supporters get in line, order their food, make the payment, get their food and go. There's so brief period to interact with the clients that the seller must nail the experience to guarantee repeat business and positive words.

Then again, there is the upside of closeness. "We cook everything before individuals, so we have a one-on-one collaboration with a client - superior to anything that we would have at a café," Raouli says.

That is the definitive explanation Fares "Freddy" Zeidaies - three-time Vendy finalist and the champion of the current year's Vendy Cup - got into the business. He has the experience of already owning a brick-and-got into café, one that generated strong business yet left him unfulfilled.

"I concluded I would not like to do it any longer," Zeidaies says. "It was not fun. It was not me. What I need is to be around the individuals, not simply around the kitchen."

So almost nine years back Zeidaies reevaluated himself as "The King of Falafel and Shawarma." He began paying rent to a stopping meter instead of a landowner. Zeidaies loyally stations his King of Falafel food truck at the same convergence in the Astoria community of Queens, serving Middle Eastern cooking. Zeidaies is undeniably progressively happy with his street activity. "I love it when they offer me that go-ahead," he says, but he likewise alerts conventional restaurateurs from naively getting into the food truck business.

Inquired as to whether customary café translates to food trucks, Zeidaies says not really. "I thought it was so comparable, but not presently," he says. "I once had a pleasant full head of hair; I was healthy. Presently I have an awful knee and I'm drained by the day's end. At a café, if you don't want to go in, you have workers or a manager who can dominate. You can call an organization and they'll send you a sous gourmet specialist. In any case, not at a street eatery."

What's more, the underlying test of finding a parking space in any case, food truck merchants must deal with the regular components. "You need to get out in the hot climate, the chilly climate," Zeidaies proceeds, which may clarify why food trucks are blasting in climate-friendly spots like Southern California.

The components are just a piece of the challenges. Gay Hughes, proprietor of the Original Mobile Tea Truck, which advanced around suburbia of Boston for a considerable length of time, really sold her truck in May 2010 and now works a fruitful extended Mobile

Tea Shoppe, a stand she sets up at ranchers' craft and markets shows.

About working the truck, Hughes says, "Every town had its very own muddled arrangement of legalities. I frequently set up at the National Park destinations because it was simpler dealing with the Federal government than the nearby organizations - that should state everything." Hughes likewise takes note of the burdensome physical demands of the activity. "All the up and down, lending and bending...Frankly, it was very hard on my body."

There are also those tight quarters to contend with. "You've got about eight feet [of space], and each person needs to man a station," Zeidaies says, explaining that his truck has one person administering the flame broil, one cooking the rice, another preparing the sauces and a fourth person covering the everything else (the sales register, packing the food, etc.). Limited space also affects the initial prep work.

"With a truck, you need to find parking, and afterward you need to prepare all your food once you arrive," Bistro Truck's Raouli says. "It takes about an hour to 90 minutes after you discover your spot."

The image Zeidaies and Raouli paint may frighten away intrigued restaurateurs. Or on the other hand, just maybe, they need to restrict their opposition, since the two of them concur that food trucks, in contrast to other fleeting fads, will stay a solid, although unusual, presence in the eatery business.

"The food truck business, if you do it well, you will be extremely fruitful," Raouli says. "We live in a city where you have intense pundits, and individuals' desires are high. The best will be here for quite a while and the most fragile will be gone before they know it."

FOOD TRUCKS, STAYING RELEVANT, AND CUSTOMER LOYALTY

When it comes to staying significant, it's imperative to realize where to plant your banner. A few people easily abide in cool, being the first to spot trends and procuring notorieties as inventive early adopters. Consider early social media evangelists or the primary individual you knew with an iPod.

At that point there are the individuals who arrive behind schedule to the party, trying energetically to drain the last drop out of an idea.

There's a major buzz circumventing food hovers about the LA Food Truck phenomenon and whether it's a waning pattern. Food trucks aren't anything new-from sandwiches to tacos, they've been blaring La Cucaracha after entering parking garages for decades.

But cook Roy Choi, founder of the Kogi truck, put another component of cool into the rolling café world when he took the Taco Truck idea (a staple on the West

Coast) and put a Korean twist on it. (Korean style meat tacos... complete and total YUM!)

His business splendidly utilizes Twitter, to declare where they'll be next and crowds structure each day for their fix. The Kogi truck has an enormous following, but a considerable amount of different foodies are duplicating everything he might do (The Grilled Cheese Truck is an incredible rage in LA among others). The imagination is amazing... but are such a large number of food trucks ruining the soup?

So that takes us back to the theme of remaining cool, relevant, and building loyalty with your clients. At the point when you're on the front line of a pattern, doing what you love, it's unadulterated delight. But out of nowhere, you have fast-food chains like Jack in the Box propelling fleets of food trucks, diluting the spirit of the movement.

Regardless of whether you're driving a food truck or selling counseling services, your ability to stand apart is the thing that will keep you top of mind.

Below are three hints to remain innovative, relevant, and #1 in your clients' eyes.

1. Constantly Keep an Eye Out for the Opportunities
   The cool individual's philosophy is to watch out for where everybody ISN'T. Be the first there and claim your spot. When the engineers show up and start placing in walkways, you realize it's time to go. For instance, Twitter was the innovation for Kogi. Presently everybody is utilizing Twitter to follow their food trucks. Is there another social media technique or mobile marketing application that can keep you upfront?

2. Thoughtfully acknowledge yourself as an innovator and founder. No, you don't prefer not to cry, "I was here first! Leave!". Or maybe, graciously greet the newcomers as though they're coming to YOUR

party. Hold the certainty of somebody who has a place anyplace you go. Your business may get some push from competitors, however, don't show your stress. This is a mentality issue... if you don't set this up, you'll go into a tailspin.

3. Develop dedication through incredible customer care service. Never let your clients and fans overlook the amount you esteem them. Give them access to the cool children club... exceptional arrangements, notices, client just rewards and so forth. Others may duplicate you all things considered, but they can't duplicate the emotional engraving you leave on your customers. They'll enthusiastically follow you wherever you go and remain faithful to you.

Chapter 7: IMPORTANCE OF SOCIAL MEDIA TO FOOD TRUCK BUSINESS

Is Social Media So Important To Food Truck Success?

Allows first get straight precisely what are the social media we're talking about. There are three I'll be covering in this part of the book, as follows:

Twitter

The Twitter revolution has always changed the landscape of versatile organizations and how they cooperate with clients. The steady stream, to and fro, of little "tweets" among clients and their preferred trucks, makes a flawlessly agreeable exchange through which the two sides significantly benefit. A decent food truck administrator doesn't deliver a talk on his items, he makes discussion, which at that point prompts the client's steady comprehension of what is being offered and why it's advantageous.

It's significant for food truck proprietors to comprehend that Twitter gives not just a chance to share their menu and location, but in addition to share fascinating stories, jokes and start drawing in discussions revolving around food. The client's hunger for a decent progressing dialogue and will re-tweet for days as more individuals voice their feeling and offer related antidotes.

Here's a recommendation: Go on Twitter, upload the name of a specific truck you'd prefer to follow, and participate in the discussions. When you feel you've gotten a decent handle on the best way to effectively "tweet," keep the accompanying tips.

1   Have a technique and stick to it. Remain steady in the style and sort of content of your "tweets."
2   Follow your kindred food truck administrators. There are a ton of smart thoughts out there.

3. Keep in touch with your clients! This can't be overemphasized. Stay constantly before your clients by tweeting each day. You don't need to be a virtuoso to do tweeting. Most times the best dialogue is made by reacting to a tweet, not by posting your own.
4. To start an account on twitter, and not keep it crisp with your tweets, resembles cooking a delicious dish, and not eating it. Remain with it!

Facebook

Facebook is another incredible social media apparatus that can advance your food truck. In contrast to Twitter, having a Facebook page enables you to go past insignificant words and rather post interesting videos and short clips about your food truck. Personally, I think posting videos where you show watchers how you set up a portion of their preferred foods is an extraordinary idea. (I doubt I'm the one in particular who isn't even somewhat intrigued by "watch us wash our food truck! So fun!" videos...)

If you have a site together with your Facebook account, interface the two! On your site have an option to "click here" and be sent to the next's page. This can build web traffic for your food truck business. Additionally, remember to utilize keywords that tie into your truck, location, and cuisine. Locate the best keywords and use em'! (A word of caution: don't overdo it or you'll get boycotted right now.)

Google+

Google+ offers food truck proprietors various tools to advance and professionalize their business. You can utilize the Google+ Events device which enables you to broadcast an event you're facilitating, finished with a start time, area and an exclusive invite rundown. You can even utilize your Gmail contacts to add to the ones you have in the Google Circle tool. After you make the event it will appear on your Google Calendar.

This specific social media gives you the alternative of talking with up to 10 individuals through the Google+ Hangout online video chat option. You can work together with individual food truck employees and acquaintances and leave "virtual sticky notes" on a "virtual whiteboard" to talk about a food truck structure or new business strategy. The alternatives are apparently endless... There are a lot of free applications that you can download to your Google+ account to improve how your business is connecting with clients.

I have included my preferred social media outlet since it deserves a chapter all to its own. The social media tool I'm alluding to is topping overviews as the "most useful, incredible social media apparatus for independent ventures." In an ongoing survey taken by the Wall Street Journal, this social media outlet was evaluated the "tool with the most potential to help," over other social media's, for example, Facebook, YouTube, and Pinterest.

Having presented the three social media, I need to share to you some secret, SOCIAL MEDIA IS FOR THE BIRDS. That is right. In such a case that you like the 98% of other entrepreneurs out there, busy in your businesses, you simply don't have the opportunity to adequately remain over all these online media services, and therefore you will give little consideration to them. I can just propose one thing. Contract somebody who is educated about food trucks and your business, to do the tweets and blogs for you.

SHOULD YOUR FOOD TRUCK START A BLOG?

Finding out precisely how to commit your time as a food truck proprietor can be troublesome - particularly if the fundamental business tasks take up most of your time and you're left with little to choose how best to help the business with trivial undertakings. One of these areas of trivial business support may appear as blogging. The key inquiry when choosing if a blog is directly for your food trailer business is figuring out how a blog can increase the value of your business and who in your group meets all requirements to write for your truck's audience.

Anyway, what can a blog accomplish for those in the food trailer industry and you particularly? Generally, blogs are an incredible method to keep your clients refreshed on the most recent news encompassing your business. This webpage utilizes posts comparative on those of Facebook and Twitter, and you may even consider connecting your blog entries from these social media sites; in any case, blogs are generally longer in length. These posts can be utilized on acquaint yourself with local people who may not be comfortable with your catering truck business and they can likewise be utilized to promote the exercises your truck is engaged with the surrounding community.

In case you're considering starting a blog, fuse it into your site. Along these lines, it's anything but difficult to discover and simple to develop, as almost certainly, your site is already up and active. You would then be able to choose whether you need your blog to be interactive or not. If it's interactive, your readers will have a choice to remark on the post with inquiries and thoughts. In spite of the fact that you may feel that discussion boards open your food trailer business to be vulnerable, there's no better method to bring out honest feedback than through the remarks and comments clients choose to leave.

Commonly, contingent upon how you build up the particular blog page, remarks can be left anonymously, which can make an increasingly open and flowing dialogue between readers. If you experience negative remarks or analysis, don't expel them from the blog website. Handle the issue in the open by requesting that the client expand (if necessary) on their negative experience and afterward offer a solution to the client.

Next, pick somebody in your group to run the blog. Regardless of whether it's you or another person, the writer must have a compelling and interesting voice that encourages readers to keep reading the posts. In order to represent your truck in a positive light on the web, guarantee that the writer utilizes appropriate spelling and grammar, and is likewise concise. You don't want your food truck's blog to be loaded up with useless information that is composed just to fill a page - which brings you to the writer's next errand: The writer must concentrate on the necessities and needs of the clients. Since the blog is being composed for the clients, it must be composed with them in mind.

Finally, when you start your blog you should stay focused on it. When you start posting updates and information, your clients will anticipate that a constant flow of news should be refreshed. The exact opposite thing you need to do is make something for your clients just to leave them disappointed by the manner in which you use it. Furthermore, don't stress, your food truck will experience enough in its daily activities to have a lot of updates for the blog webpage to thrive on.

Chapter 8: BENEFITS OF STARTING A FOOD TRUCK VENTURE

Today, the quick development of the food business is for all to see. Food is fundamental, we as a whole realize that clearly however in the most recent decade or somewhere in the vicinity, the business of hotels and restaurants has taken off enormously. We as a whole love to eat out with our loved ones at least once or twice per week and if the quality of food is acceptable, cash isn't a concern for most of us.

Starting a business

Restaurants and conventional eateries have always been there and will be Conventional eateries and restaurants have constantly been there and will be noticeable for a long time to come. Be that as it may, food trucks are the most recent pattern and individuals love the way that they would now be able to get hygienic, healthy, and delicious dishes without going to expensive eateries. If you are considering starting your own food truck, it very well may be inconceivably remunerating just as challenging. With the developing notoriety of these "restaurant on wheels", it is basic to make your vehicle stand apart from the rest.

Advantages

- **Low investment:** One of the greatest advantages of starting this sort of venture is the fact that they require incredibly low starting investment and working expenses. Contrasted with running an eatery, this sort of business is far less expensive to run. For the first time business visionaries who are simply making their first strides in this business, this is an extraordinary endeavor for gaining experience for what's to come. For effectively established organizations, this is an extraordinary endeavor for growing the income streams and market for more customers.

- **Dynamic:** Working in an eatery can be a bit exhausting in light of the fact, not every time will they have a full house. Individuals who appreciate a clamoring working condition, this sort of business are apt for them. With individuals coming and going throughout the day, one would once in a while have a dull minute in these vehicles.

- **Freedom to experiment**: In normal eateries, you simply need to adhere to specific plans; there is almost no space for experimenting. Proprietors of a mobile restaurant business can modify with their dishes once in a while and produce new menus a lot speedier. This aides in astonishing individuals who love to eat new colorful dishes and not adhere to the ordinary ones.

- **Participation in occasions:** With eateries, you can't really take an interest in popular occasions around the city and that is likely probably the greatest disadvantage. With mobile restaurants, you can take them anywhere you feel like. For example, if there is a huge reasonable going on in some piece of the city where you want to draw in new customers, you can rapidly head to the spot and start serving.

As a general rule, individuals are excessively with the response about they will get in this sort of venture, however, in all honesty, you won't get achievement overnight. You must show patience about it and sit tight for your opportunity.

THREE GREAT REASONS TO OPEN A FOOD TRUCK

The street food development has picked up fame in the course of the most recent couple of years, and if you've eaten from one recently, you will understand why. Street food is delightful, (typically) modest, and helpful for the client. Even TV is getting in on the act with programming highlighting road merchants in The Great Food Truck Race airing on the Food Network. If you are reading this, at that point you are most likely keen on getting involved by beginning a mobile food business of your own. So we should investigate the main reasons why starting a 'roach coach' can be a brilliant and remunerating adventure!

A truck can go to where the clients are.

This may not appear that enormous of an arrangement, however, it's perhaps the greatest advantages to operating a food truck. Generally, customary cafés can only service residents that are in the encompassing zone. Accordingly, it turns out to be subject to that individual community. Moreover, there are ordinarily numerous other contending cafés in that same territory to contend with. With a mobile food business, you are not constrained to one neighborhood, you can hit a wide range of various regions, you can set up at community occasions like sporting events or festivals, attend outdoor foodie occasions or set up late-night outside of night clubs and bars. Basically, it offers you much greater flexibility as far as locations and times where you can offer food to clients.

Compared to an independent restaurant, overhead expenses are much lower.

It is considerably less costly to set up a food truck versus setting up a new café/restaurant and all the related costs that accompany it. For instance, lease, build-out, and operating expenses. Since you are regularly paying for more workers and a physical structure your overhead costs are just that much higher.

Serving extraordinary food that makes clients happy will bring a grin to your face

This is maybe the most significant part of running this sort of business. A decent mobile food business can profit around $75-150,000 per year, not a huge amount of cash. But if you are serving food around an idea and menu that you have endeavored to create and truly have faith in, while building relationships with the community around you, it will make the endeavor all worthwhile. Likewise, food trucks are ready for advertising via social media. The demographic of client tends to be a more youthful, urban crowd, who are very much associated through social media. Building a loyal following through promoting and branding utilizing Facebook and Twitter is free and fun. Food trucks have been a continuous pattern for quite a long while on both the east coast and west coast (and west coast specifically because of their atmosphere) but the two coasts have gernered a youthful and dynamic crowd that have embraced food truck and road food contributions as one of a kind, trendy and vogue.

Chapter 9: HOW TO GET CUSTOMERS TO YOUR FOOD TRUCK

One of the top ten inquiries individuals beginning a mobile food truck ask is "How would I get clients to my truck?" Many new administrators, unfortunately, believe that if you build it they will come. That might be valid in certain conditions, however, it's not a genuine business strategy.

The uplifting news here is that it truly doesn't cost a great deal of upright cash to get moving.

But at the present time, we should concentrate on a couple of social media advertising thoughts. Most mobile trucks can direct people to their organizations utilizing social media. Truth be told I am persuaded this is one of the significant reasons the mobile food truck segment has exploded.

BELOW ARE FOUR THINGS YOU MUST DO!

1. Set up a fan page on Facebook for your truck. This is extremely easy to do. Ensure your logo is on the page and that you include video and photographs of your truck.
2. Create a twitter page. Twitter is regularly the communication platform for the under 30 group. When it's set up start building your fan base.
3. Create a foursquare account and enable individuals on foursquare to follow you.
4. Set up a Flickr and YouTube account to post photos and videos.
5. I didn't intend to truly provide you with a $ 5, however, this discussion would not be complete without at least referencing that you MUST have your own site too.

These are the fundamental strategies at this very moment. Each cost nothing to do and is exceptionally effective. Ensure your truck and the entirety of your promoting materials have your Facebook and Twitter addresses on them. One of the large issues with social media is that it is continually advancing and evolving. Ensure you stay up to date on the most recent trends.

QUALITIES THAT A FOOD TRUCK VENDOR MUST HAVE

In the past, individuals thought of food trucks as a source of junk food. Anyway as time passed by, the value and the functionality of food trucks have been uncovered. Individuals who are swamped at work and have no opportunity to take their lunch in the solaces of their homes or eateries rely on food truck proprietors to bring them healthy meals.

In view of the notoriety of vending trucks, few people who might need to earn are venturing to this kind of business. If you wish to be a successful food truck trader, you should have the following attitudes:

Patient. Finding a vehicle that you can transform into a vending truck involves a great deal of time. There are a lot of organizations who sell vehicles that are perfect for being converted into food trucks. If you lack the patience in scouring the market for the best deal that you can get, at that point, you might be deceived by merchants who take advantage of the high demand for vehicles. If you need to set aside cash and get the best vehicle you should be able to look for the best deal.

Hard-working. A food seller should be productive. Being innovative means being to get the same number of requests as you can from the workplaces that are situated at places where your food truck will pass on. If the seller is innovative, then he will be able to convey his products to numerous workplaces and offices.

Friendly. It is significant that you can assemble affinity with your clients. This is because if they consider you to be a well-known face and a businessperson who considers nothing but profits. Friendliness means you selling a greater amount of your merchandise and items.

Creative. Clients don't care for routine food. This is the reason why they would avoid heading off to the office cafeteria to eat their meals. You should be creative in your menus. Ensure that you have an assortment of food that you can offer to your clients. It won't just satisfy your clients, however, you will likewise be able to remain in front of your competition.

Manage time successfully. You should recall that the basic reason why you are starting a food truck business is for the adaptability and freedom rather than simply being positioned in one location. If you can manage your time well, then you can serve numerous clients. The more places you can visit in one day, the more clients you, the more profits you gain.

The food truck business is anything but a difficult business to learn. If you have every one of these attributes, then you will unquestionably become wildly successful.

TIPS ON PLANNING A MENU FOR YOUR FOOD TRUCK

Food trucks are famous sights in places close to construction sites and government offices. This is on the grounds that individuals working in construction sites and offices have a hectic timetable in this way not leaving them much time for lunch. A food truck business is a simple business to work once you have obtained all the gear that you need. The most tiresome part of this business, however, is planning a menu. You should consistently ensure that the menu you offer your regular clients are those that pass their sense of taste and their fulfillment. In this business, it is significant for you to realize which kinds of menu are effectively sold. Below is a few hints on the best way to plan a menu for your food truck.

If you know somebody who knows a ton about what individuals do and don't eat in the area where you would need your truck to cruise by, don't hesitate to approach them for menu recommendations. It is additionally significant for you to consider the kind of individuals you will serve. It will help your business a great deal if you know the nationality and the eating inclinations of the individuals that work on the route that you wish to take. This is essential to your menu planning since this will assist you with settling on what to sell and what not to offer to them.

Besides the cooked meals that you want to purchase, it is likewise prudent for you to sell fast foods, for example, sandwiches. You can contact a commissary specialist that is found on your route. This commissary specialist can give you some sandwich ideas.

Tweak your menu relying upon the time of day that you will be passing your route. Fried eggs, pastries, and bacon can be a decent menu that you can take when you are serving breakfast. In the afternoon, your clients will be searching for light food so it is suggested that you serve them sandwiches and various kinds of snacks that come along with a cold drink. If you wish to work until the night time, pick a healthy meal, for example, meat or chicken dishes or some pureed potatoes and sauce. This will go as a complete hearty meal. You can likewise serve coleslaw and buttered vegetables as fixings. Ensure that the fixings you offer vary every day. Along these lines, your clients won't get bored with your truck options.

These are just a few hints on the most proficient method to plan a menu. In planning a menu you should think about two significant things: consumer loyalty and assortment. When you have fulfilled these two things then you make certain to have clients hanging tight for you to pass and you're certain to earn a lot.

Chapter 10: REASONS WHY FOOD TRUCKS ARE HOT RIGHT NOW

From Los Angeles to New York, street food is everywhere. Projections recommend that by 2020 food trucks will be a billion-dollar industry. Since 2009 the food truck business has become 80%. Food trucks are setting deep roots and here's twenty reasons why this trend is so hot.

1 Changing Perceptions

Gone are the days when mobile kitchens were classified as "Roach Coaches". Individuals comprehend that street food businesses are held to the same (in some cases higher) sanitation and safety standards of any café.

2 Value

Lunch wagons give an economical meal for the frugal foodie. Generally, street food is more affordable than conventional feasting alternatives

3 Social Media

Chuckwagon operators are bosses of computerized communication and they use it to drive deals. Their tweets, Pinterest entries, blogs, and Facebook pages are continually developing promoting platforms that people, in general, has embraced.

4 Lower Overhead

Mobile kitchens have a less expensive working expense than physical cafés. With no lease to pay or building to help, food trucks can run a lean and rewarding activity less expensive than their conventional eating rivals.

5 Lower Startup Cost

To open a fixed area eatery expects a few times the measure of capital than it does to begin a food truck.

Reasonably a business person with $75,000 could have a working food truck business.

6 Location, Location, Location

The mobility of a chow wagon gives the proprietor the opportunity to change his site day by day, even like clockwork if the event that he so picks. That pizza shop that you go to can't drive their building to fairs, events, and festivals.

7 Cooperation

Lunch wagon administrators are a very close network that works together so everybody profits by every other business. One food truck parked on the street may go unnoticed by a hungry lunch crowd. Four food trucks on a corner makes a scene.

8 Marketing

A major rig is a moving billboard. Every time they are out and about they are publicizing. Seeing a fiercely hued step van shrouded with logos in a business region creates buzz and drives deals.

9 Fast Food

You need your lunch hot and quick? A food truck gives time-starved diners a fast bite without the waiting uptime of a sit-down café.

10 Healthy Options

A ton of mobile kitchens are serving hot dogs and deep-fried candy but many are serving veggie-lover, gluten-free and vegan meals to cater to healthy tastes. Some food trucks have gone so far as just serving healthy choices.

11 Choices

Consumers like choices. A couple of food trucks parked on the road give hungry individuals a especially custom-tailored menu where they can blend and match their feast as per their preferences. You can have dim entirety for an appetizer, stroll over to another truck and get burritos and in case you're still hungry, check out a yogurt truck.

12 Culture

Each possible ethnic, cooking style, and provincial food are represented by food trucks. Buyers can eat Maine lobster on the west coast of California food on the east coast. Diners can delve into Korean, French, Italian, Thai, Greek, Ethiopian, Japanese or American food. In case you're a food truck follower, anything is possible for you.

13 Fusion Flavors

Japanese tacos? Yes. German Gyros? Expedite it. Mexican Pizza? More, please. Imaginative chefs are pushing the combination envelope to make unique, fascinating and delicious offerings to delight adventurous foodies.

14 The Fame Game

Spike Mendelsohn, Tom Colicchio, Jose Andres, and Jamie Oliver have run food trucks. Some well-known Chefs utilize mobile kitchens to test recipes and concepts for their cafés. Food trucks enable VIP Chefs to explore different avenues regarding plans without risk and reach a more extensive market. This trend will proceed in light of the fact that individuals love superstars.

15 Fun Factor

Street food is a cheap excitement option. Proprietors attempt to offer an enjoyable feasting experience to their customers in the city. Workers can get away from their cubicle and experience a festival like environment on their launch-day break. The brilliantly shaded rigs are fun, the food is fun and the people taking your order are fun.

16 The American Dream

Socially conscious foodies comprehend that road food merchants give jobs and a community at large in the cities where they run. Individuals are all the more ready to give their well-deserved money to a local business proprietor than a faceless corporation. Street food merchants additionally boost deals in the retail territories where they work. If your retail business is slacking, consider inviting a food truck to your business.

17 Fresh Air

When the weather is charming, nothing is superior to getting outside. A snappy walk in the recreation center to a lunch wagon is what the doctor ordered to lift the spirits of eaters in the solid jungle. Who wants leftover

Chinese in the workplace that you go through 50 hours every week?

18 Novelty

From the developing menu alternatives to new units on the scene, food trucks present a novel approach to eating out. Mobile cooking gives a fascinating eating niche to customers who have become tired of being continually blasted by messages from chain cafés and corporate fast food.

19 Fresh and Local

Mobile kitchens are bringing the farm to table idea to urban communities over the world. Chefs are purchasing proteins, dairy and produce from neighborhood sources and creating preferable food than some brick and mortar eateries. Customers can taste the distinction between those small scale greens grown down the road when contrasted with the salad processed in factory several miles away.

20 Street Food Tastes Good

Regardless of whether it's a escargot or burger, road Chefs are making astonishing suppers. The assortment, quality and deliciousness of mobile food is faltering and embraced by the world. From appetizing, upscale meals to artery clogging deep-fried, street food tastes great and therefore, food trucks are here to stay.

Chapter 11: THE ANATOMY OF FOOD TRUCKS - FAST FOOD JUST GOT FASTER

One approach to entice our taste buds that is recently seeing more press is the food truck. A café/restaurant on wheels, this idea is gradually sweeping individuals' stomachs and imaginations. Transforming mobile cooking into an art form, food trucks over the world are making feeding furors, eating transformations and fanatical followings.

Through social media apparatuses, for example, Twitter and increased mainstream exposure word is spreading rapidly about how fun, delectable and convenient these mobile restaurants truly are. As more and more of these mobile food wagons enter the market the quality and choice just stand to improve and advance, which makes this freshly discovered method for eating much progressively captivating. In this part of the book, we will take a look at a couple of the more well-known food trucks and afterward turn out a portion of the segments that make up an effective food transportation activity.

A typical theme all through the food truck industry is specialty cooking. Most trucks have niche corners of cooking and to a great extent center around serving specific kinds of food. Regularly constrained by space, time and cost these wheeled machines try to stamp their brand and identities themselves by giving a food product and service not normally accessible in a standard café setting. A couple of traveling culinary concoctions that truly outline the importance of these trucks incorporate The Nom Truck (Banh Mi) in Los Angeles and The Grilled Cheese Truck (sandwiches), Slidin' Thru (sliders) of Las Vegas popularity and Schnitzel and Things (fried meat and breaded) and Wafels and Dinges both representing New York City.

Even the remote and exotic like the Kahuku Shrimp Truck in Hawaii are gaining more reputation.

If you do choose to visit one later on, here are a couple of the embellishments they will use to provide your sustenance.

Past the real trucks, inspections, and licenses that can change considerably, there are a couple of nuts and bolts to pretty much every activity. Proper food trucks should have a stainless steel sink assigned for hand washing. A separate compartment segmented sink for washing utensils, vegetables and to cover some other washing needs. There ought to be storage compartments conducive to keeping products fresh and cold if necessary like refrigerators, ice baths and freezers. Storage territories will likewise be utilized for provisions and business items too. A clean cutting and food planning counter is required. There should be room made for instruments, for example, fryers, grills and toasters as well. An effectively accessible serving window is another key that must not be disregarded. Extras that for the most part balance well-known food wagons are covers and fixing counters, computer correspondence and strategic client interaction.

Food trucks are an intriguing new twist on the feasting experience and the boom gives little indication of going bust anytime soon. Now is a fabulous time to hitch a ride on this culinary bandwagon.

AN AMAZING CONCEPT CALLED FOOD TRUCKS

In our bustling lives, most of us don't get the time and opportunity to cook at home. Getting a meal while in transit to office or in transit back home is a simple way out. In any case, takeaways at huge eateries pinch the pocket and side of the road junk food takes on one's wellbeing.

Food trucks are a great solution for all those who do not know how to cook, who hate cooking, and those who have no time for it!

Fundamentally, these vehicles are mobile kitchens. While a portion of these have plans for cooking, others may sell pre-packaged food or frozen products, for example, desserts. Those with in-built kitchens, cook from scratch, which incorporates preparing, chopping, cooking, and serving. Fast food trucks selling French fries, burgers, sandwiches, and other things are hot-top picks. Be that as it may, proprietors of these mobile eateries are exploring different avenues regarding different cooking styles as well.

This idea is mainstream in numerous parts of the world. Individuals now pre-book these vehicles to cater to various occasions, for example, parties, carnivals, sporting and much more. These are regular in workplaces and school grounds as well.

Starting a Food Truck Business:

It might sound simple to set up this business, but, similar to any other endeavor, it requires planning, as well as unique abilities.

Initially, a permit from the concerned division should be secured. Various urban communities have various guidelines and regulations. One would require declarations from the health division, a permit from the trade authorities to do this business, agree to drive the business truck, and check the parking limitations.

The subsequent step is to choose what one wishes to sell and would it require cooking onboard. The acquisition of the vehicle would rely upon this. Many driving carmakers are producing these trucks. The business visionary needs to settle on the decision dependent on his prerequisite and budget.

Financial institutions would give loans for this endeavor. The individuals who wish to apply for a loan may build up a fund plan.

The following step is to purchase equipment, take on lease a private parking spot, get associated with providers, and discover a customer database. Promoting/Marketing is a significant part of this business. There would be numerous takers for this idea; one simply needs to connect with the intended interest group.

There is a variety of large names in this industry. The remarkable ones include Florida, Big Gay Ice Cream Truck in New York City, Chef Jeremiah for Miami, Devilicious Food Truck in San Diego, Sarah's Cake Stop in St. Louis, Missouri, California, Chi'Lantro BBQ in Texas, and Clover Food Lab in Boston, Massachusetts.

FOOD TRUCKS VS RESTAURANTS ON THE ENVIRONMENT

Which of the two are more environmentally friendly, or is there basically no conclusive answer? At the present time, there are numerous people that may rapidly accept that food trucks are the more regrettable of the two evils of national focus on how naturally economical practices tie to methods of transportation.

However, sustainability is something that becomes an integral factor at whatever point a light is turned on, plastic is tossed into the trash, dishes are washed, and so forth. Environmentally friendly (or destructive) practices don't begin and stop with the key in the ignition, however, they rather occur during and after every single working hour of a business - in a food trailer or in a customary physical café.

How about we take a look at the components that become possibly the most important factor during these business tasks.

The location. As you most likely are aware, catering trucks are mobile. They move all around and subsequently leave a smaller impression on where they've been. There's little framework, besides the business kitchen, that should be kept up. And afterward, there are eateries. Cafés have numerous huge areas that must be lit up, cleaned regularly and temperature-regulated. These physical elements exist constantly, not simply during working hours.

Energy Use. As referenced above, a conventional café's physical area makes the requirement for electricity and natural gas to keep up comfortable temperatures, and to give light to eating clients. In the kitchens, cooking is commonly done with natural gas, and frying pans and stoves are kept hot during the working hours. As per the 2003 Commercial Building Energy Consumption

Survey, most eateries utilize 38.4kWh of electricity per square foot every year, which is roughly 77,000 kWh every year for a 2,000 ft2 eatery.

Food trucks likewise require a heat source for cooking, so they commonly use propane. During a year, a normal food trailer will utilize around 900 gallons of propane a year, in addition, fuel prerequisites for driving around. In spite of the fact that this fuel is generally diesel or gas, catering trucks may likewise utilize biodiesel or vegetable oil. Besides, an onboard generator addresses electricity issues. While generators are normally more polluting than grid-provided power, food trailers demand less power and depend more on natural light.

Vehicle miles. In spite of the fact that restaurants can't pile on miles going to clients, their clients are most likely traveling to get to these customary eateries. Basically, a short outing by a food truck can frequently counterbalance various little excursions by clients that would have generally driven to an eatery.

Waste. For the waste component in the food business, it's a tie between food trucks and eateries. While some catering trucks are considered eco-friendly by utilizing corn-based plastic, bagasse, or reused paper takeout compartments, despite everything they're making squanders. Conversely, eateries can utilize reusable plates, cups, and utensils; be that as it may, take-out and fast food eateries frequently depend vigorously on take-out containers that are made of Styrofoam and plastic.

Is the winner clear yet? From this subjective analysis, clearly, mobile food stands generally produce less hurtful ecological effects. Obviously, it is completely conceivable that a few eateries will be more sustainable than other food trailers.

Keep in mind, as a food truck proprietor you should pay attention to your clients' interests. Your enthusiasm for ecological practices will hold steadfast followers and pull in new clients to your business.

MAINTAINING YOUR FOOD TRUCK IN THE WINTER

Half of the nation is encountering freezing cool, harsh climate during this part of the year. This is particularly noteworthy for organizations that partially or entirely rely upon climate conditions for deals. What's more, regardless of whether these businesses can discover approaches to keep deals up while they persevere through the chilly, they additionally need to keep up the working hardware that spends long periods of time outside.

Food trucks are no special case to this standard. Just like with vehicles, truck proprietors continually run into challenges with firing up the engine in the cold conditions. In spite of the fact that you and other catering truck proprietors should expect to set up your trucks before the winter season begins, if you haven't there are still simple approaches to do maintenance jobs and safety checks that are explicit to chilled air and winter driving before the end of the season. Here are a couple of steps to guaranteeing that your mobile food stand endures the through the rest of the season:

Ensure your normal upkeep is up to date. If you do this during the snowy season, you can help ensure that you don't experience unforeseen repairs.

Take a look at your antifreeze. To help protect your food vehicle, ensure that your truck contains a full degree of 50/50 blend of antifreeze and water all through the season. You can get this investigated at a service station or test it yourself the proper device.

Check your tires. Winter isn't a simple season on your tires. On a cold highway, these are the most significant highlights among you and the guard rails. The National Highway Transportation Safety Board reports that you need at least 2/32" of profundity to be protected. What's more, check your tire strain to ensure that you're altogether siphoned up - tires will, in general, lose pressure in the cold.

Review and replace your wipers. Your wipers are even progressively susceptible to damage when you and your food trailer's group are continually utilizing them to remove ice, debris, snow, and hail the windshield. When you're driving, you rely upon your wipers to clear anything from your vision that is laying on the exterior, so it's basic to ensure they can carry out their responsibility. In the winter it turns out to be considerably progressively essential to focus on your catering food truck's wipers as your truck will encounter sand and salt from the highway department's snow cleanup schedule.

Watch out for your windshield washer liquid. It's a tendency for vehicle proprietors to utilize an abundance of washer liquid to help melt ice from the windshield of their food trucks' in the winter. As this is the situation, ensure that you check and replace your washer liquid.

Proceed with your yearly upkeep as necessary, in addition to your winter maintenance. So as to ensure that you're food trailer is performing well all year, you should normally clean your battery posts, examine your spark plug wires, investigate your brakes, and check your motor oil.

Complete these undertakings throughout the winter season so your food truck and its passengers can be as prepared and safe in the cold weather as possible. Try not to let this season put you out of commission!

Chapter 12: INCORPORATING FOOD TRUCKS INTO PRIVATE PARTY CATERING

Catering has been around for quite a while. The most customary methods for catering were nearby or off-site. Caterers either prepared the food right at the occasion or they carried the cooked food to the occasion. These were the conventional ways cooks would give their party catering food services. Today, there are increasingly more food truck cooks offering catering services for parties and other occasions.

Food trucks are one of the recent trends in the food business; with most average size urban areas having the trucks pop up on every street corner. From pulled-pork sandwiches to vegan offering, the cool thing about these trucks is the wide exhibit of ethnic portions that they offer.

While the food truck trend has been on the ascent, there have likewise been a few difficulties, for example, city guidelines and regulations, as well as operators getting being incredibly strict with respect to parking. In spite of the huge influx of clients, truck administrators are considering some fresh possibilities and addressing where they can go somewhere else. Food truck administrators are presently moving into the party catering business. A lot of trucks are taking advantage of the wedding business, as they can deliver a ton of food for the guests and with food trucks being so in vogue and new in the party catering business, what could be cooler than having a truck cook the food on the greatest day of your life?

If you are setting up a party for an upcoming occasion, for example, an anniversary, engagement or wedding, there are a couple of tips you can follow while hiring a food truck as your party catering service.

1. If you are having it at your home, be a decent neighbor and let them know about the upcoming party. They will be appreciative for the heads up.
2. Set up traffic cones before and behind the truck with the goal that people are aware of its presence. (Not that you wouldn't be able to see in any case!)
3. Talk with the food truck service and ensure the person in question can make a wide range of dishes, including vegan and vegan options. Your guests will be grateful.
4. Be sure you have hungry guests!

Following these pointers will support you if you choose to follow the "food truck as a cook" pattern. It likewise ends up being a financially savvy path for party catering, and with insignificant work and personnel included, you have a more noteworthy assortment of food at a lower cost. What's more, with the manner in which things have been with the economy, cheaper, and simple cheaper choices are good.

SPECIALIZED INSURANCE FOR THE FOOD STREET VENDOR AND FOOD TRUCK

You may consider them the moving food store, much like a café, restaurant or bistro without walls and locality permanence. To the insurance companies, the food road seller that shows their delicacies on the other side or curb or along the road just as the food truck that movements from worksite to business site so as to cater for hungry patrons outside are both in their very own business class in terms of indemnity coverage.

With a certain risk exposure that separates every one of these industry businesses from the snack retail outlet or the standard food, the food road seller and food truck needs their very own particular insurance strategy, customized expressly to the different risks they face on an everyday premise.

What kind of business coverage do the mobile food shops, for example, the road seller and food truck really require? The accompanying outlines the essential points being referred to.

Food Street Vendor

Pre-arranged to business interests, the urban communities, towns and numerous regions that dot the national guide disperse licenses to allow road dealers that offer prepared food and natural product to passing pedestrians on streets, lanes and walkways. Delicious tastes, presentation, and smells entice passersby with their offering of pizza, tacos, hot pretzels, French fries, hot dogs, subs, etc. Related insurance coverage incorporates property, stock, supply, general risk, auto liability and products liability. Related and coverage premiums, however, are custom-made to the individual seller through any of the related nation-wide insurance agencies to improve and tweak commercial security.

Food Serving Truck

Like the street seller but with its own arrangement of individualized coverage needs because of its method of truck commute, the food serving truck is likewise outfitted with a city, town, or city license to operate. Giving a full menu of cold and hot food and snacks to its ravenous clients, the food truck requires the protection coverage of the merchant and more: property, stock, supply, products liability, general liability, auto liability, just as the real truck insurance coverage.

Obviously, interested individuals are best off digging further into the related insurance matter with an expert that has their eventual benefits at the top of the priority list and can make the person in question into an educated insurance customer.

NEW YORK FOOD TRUCKS FOR HAPPY EATING

Food trucks have become a staple of New York. You can't walk more than two blocks without seeing somebody offering food in a little white holder. Dutch settlers introduced pushcart food in 1691 initially. The food probably won't have been as delectable in those days, however, it was a simple method to get a brisk bute during your mid-day break.

The food has changed, however, the idea remains the same. New Yorkers are occupied individuals and nobody has the time to sit down in an eatery and have lunch. New York food trucks have and consistently will cater to the lunch crowd. Rather than making do with a chicken, rice, or hotdog you can appreciate gourmet dinners - everything from waffles to tacos to dumplings. It is all excellent food; thus the long queues folded over the block. There are a lot of incredible trucks to attempt, however, let us talk about certain trucks you can't pass up.

Everybody realizes breakfast can be eaten any time of day. If you understand how astonishing waffles are, look at Waffles and Dinges. Get it? The "Dinges," incorporate dulce de leche, Belgian chocolate fudge, pecans, bananas, whipped cream, and so forth. Furthermore, remember the scoop of vanilla frozen yogurt! What sort of waffle would it be? Other than the customary sweet waffles, there is an appetizing waffle, however, it is just for the adventurous. It has pulled BBQ pork and coleslaw slathered on top. Try it before you judge!

Prefer BBQ without the waffle? At that point head over to Korilla BBQ, a food truck serving "classic Korean recipes in contemporary structures." Choose a filling, for example, chicken thighs, rib-eye, pulled pork, or tofu and afterward stick it in a burrito, Chosun bowl, or tacos. At that point obviously, you can add on some kimchi, cheddar, salsa hot sauce, and other ingredients.

Not in the mood for zesty kimchi? Maybe a customary Greek food truck would better fill your stomach. Souvlaki GR food truck is so staggeringly scrumptious that they presently have a café on the Lower East Side. Other than the standard pita souvlaki, you can likewise feast on a Greek burger, salad, fries, and choco-freta - a Greek chocolate wafer bar. Sometimes the basic food is simply the best!

The choices don't stop there, there is Bistro Truck serving Mediterranean cooking, Big D's Grub Truck dishing out grinder and tacos sandwiches, Rickshaw Dumpling Truck steaming dumplings (what else?), so much more. NYC food trucks have become an incredible marvel. When your stomach is grumbling, stop by one of these astonishing trucks for some grub.

Chapter 13: REASONS WHY YOUR BUSINESS OR CHARITY SHOULD PARTNER WITH A FOOD TRUCK

Regardless of whether you are the leader of a charity fundraiser, the CEO of a global enterprise or an entrepreneur, there are numerous reasons why partnering together with a food truck may be good for your undertaking.

Whether you will likely propel your organization's marketing, fund-raise for your school's athletic department or boost deals at your business, food trucks give a one of a kind chance to custom tailor your company's objectives.

1. Mobile Kitchens create a buzz. Are sales slacking at your used vehicle lot? Are worried about getting enough income for your fundraiser? A giant

splendidly hued food truck at your occasion drives individuals' interest and builds potential clients or donors to your occasion. Combined with a radio station, a chow wagon may be exactly what you have to arrive at your deals or fundraising objectives.

2   Food Truck administrators are experts in social media. Facebook, Twitter and the web are the instruments of a mobile kitchen's trade and they have faithful followers. If those followers realize that their preferred lunch wagon is selling food at your business, numerous individuals will go to your business and be more receptive to your attempt to sell something. Tae advantage of mobile food truck's social media presence and fans to boost your deals.

3   Economics. Having a mobile kitchen at your occasion is reasonable and as modest as asking if their truck is available for your occasion. Let a food

truck set up in your parking area close to your entrance. If you have a little money that you would contribute you could work an arrangement with the food truck where you pay for the initial 50 meals for your initial 50 clients. Clients love giveaways. Individuals like free stuff and you can give them something fun, unique and thoughtful that won't burn up all available resources. If you are doing a magnanimous charitable fundraiser, most food trucks will gladly go to your occasion for free and many will give you a percentage of their deals for the benefit of being at your occasion.

4. Consider a sponsorship. Numerous upstart lunch wagons will put your organization's name, logo, web address, and telephone number on their truck at a cost. It doesn't need to cost thousands of dollars either. A few administrators will place your data on their truck for free or discounted services and goods. Negotiate to have your information close to the

menu where every one of the people is. A huge number of individuals will see your ads. Most mobile kitchen proprietors would be respected to put your charity's logo on their truck for free.

5. Consider an organization partnership. If you possess a carport, offer a mobile kitchen proprietor free oil changes or investigations in return for placing something on the truck that states "Carport Services for XYZ food truck provided by your carport name". The organization concept is extremely constrained to your creative mind. Own a brewery? Own a supermarket? Give the truck proprietors the choice to utilize your items at a marked down cost in return for your brew or items being utilized and cited directly in their menu. Any business can cooperate with a truck and everybody included will profit by the relationship. The mobile kitchen proprietor reduces working, food or upkeep costs while the business providing the discount, item or

service gets huge amounts of modest exposure and brand acknowledgment.

6. Your workers need a break. A catered occasion at your place of business will boost morale. If your business can't bear to pay for your employee's lunch, locate a mobile kitchen that serves incredible food and consider one day monthly as food truck day. Have a food truck visit your business on a set day and at noon, watch the grins on your employee's faces.

7. Have a challenge. If your business is slacking, offer a catered food truck occasion as a prize for your business team. Whoever sells the most wins a free party at their home for 30 individuals. At costs as low as 10 dollars for every individual, that 300 dollars that you contributed could truly pump up your sales group and propel them to boost your profits. Everybody loves a free party.

8   Gift promotions, certificates, and coupons. Work a deal with a well-known food truck where you print up coupons or vouchers offering two dollars off a feast at the truck. Whatever the presumptive worth of the voucher is offer to cover the first part. Offer the vouchers or coupons to clients who purchase your items or service. The mobile kitchen profits by expanded deals and your clients will appreciate the impetus plus you are increasing a client's loyalty.

9   Let them park in your parcel on your slowest deals day, once I seven days. Food trucks are continually searching for spots to sell food and there is no reason whatsoever your business can't profit by this. This relationship is extraordinary for retail deals, however, it could apply to services or media outlets too. You aren't constrained to one truck either. When clients discover that each Tuesday at noon there is a food truck at your business, there will be a relentless increment of traffic at your store. Promote

"Food Truck Tuesdays" with flyers in your store alongside information via social media and your site page. A similar idea applies to brick and mortar charitable organizations.

10. If you can't beat them go along with them. Offer a food truck the chance to give gift coupons, giveaways, and certificates from your business in return for exposure in your business. The relationship could be as basic as permitting the food truck to hang flyers in your retail space and you give a link to the food truck's web address from your site page. The mobile kitchen passes out your flyers or coupons at their next large occasion for the exposure that you give them and your advancement reaches a totally new audience.

FOOD TRUCKS: THE REAL MOVABLE FEASTS

From the basic chuck wagon fare of stews, biscuit, and beans, we have progressed significantly and expect far more than the old cellophane wrapped sandwich of the 50s and 60s, alongside stale coffee. Ethnic cooking styles and specially made hot foods are presently typical for harried on-the-run office workers, and we're willing to pay as much as possible for the comfort.

During the 50s, mobile canteens serviced U.S. Armed force troops on bases and maneuvers, however, they were little more than guideline chow. Americans have generally expected far more and innovative merchants happily answer the call. From early frozen yogurt trucks to the hot dog merchants with their Vienna Beef umbrellas, thousands tumble out of workplaces, plants and stores, went to that truck down the road where they know what they'll discover and wouldn't mind remaining in line for it. Who needs stale candy machine foods or fast food burgers when we can get new falafel pressed into pita bread, a plate of nachos or a true fish and chips wrapped in newsprint. What has advanced from the "roach coach" of the past to a scene that propelled the career of numerous official cooks, food trucks currently even provide food at unique occasions, school campuses, weddings and conferences?

How about we inspect the most well known and most recent offerings from these meals-on-wheels across the country. The vast majority of these truck administrators additionally have eateries various areas, and many are culinary school graduate and chefs:

The Grilled Cheeserie - from essential to architect grilled cheese sandwiches, Nashville

The Taco Truck - an assortment of tacos and fixings, just as burritos, Hoboken, NJ

Fukuburger Truck - the real last name of its Japanese owner, burgers highlight bizarre Asian garnishes and sauces, Las Vegas

Macintosh Mart Truck - takes cheese and mac to another level with innovative fixings, Philadelphia

Luke's Lobster - lobster, crab and shrimp rolls for about 17USD (obviously not for those on a financial limit) New York City

The Cow and Curd – batter-dipped, cheese curds, and deep-fried, with plunging sauces, Philadelphia

Kogi BBQ - inventive and diverse Korean food, Los Angeles

Ms. Cheezious - more designer grilled cheddar sandwiches, one of America's preferred comfort foods, Miami

Cinnamon Snail - vegetarian food for the more health-cognizant and meat-eating crowd, with not a snail in sight (go figure) NYC

Moo BBQ and Oink - award-winning pork and beef BBQ with every one of the trimmings, NJ

If you venture into ethnic neighborhoods, for example, a major city Chinatown, clearly you'll discover a dominance of their local foods dabbing the streets, yet in general, these are the most widely recognized menu across the country:

- Hamburgers
- Hot dogs
- Barbecue
- Smoothies / healthy drinks and juices
- "Grown-up" grilled cheese sandwiches
- Sliders
- Coffee and coffee drinks
- Cupcakes and desserts
- Lobster rolls
- Mediterranean menus / Gyros
- Crepes with special toppings
- Street tacos and burritos
- Sushi

- Vietnamese Banh Mi sandwiches
- Pizza
- Ice cream and soft serve
- Shaved ice / Italian ice
- Indian food
- Hawaiian food
- Chicken wings

In the US, food trucks are a $1.2 billion industry. Regardless of the undeniable difficulties, for example, absence of hot running water, strict guidelines, health and licensing laws, food trucks serve a significant role in our general public and give an indispensable help to a huge number of workers all over the place. In spite of the fact that chuck wagons may essentially be nostalgia, the idea lives on. Food trucks. At the point when you just can hardly wait to eat.

FOOD TRUCKS AND NACHOS

Food trucks were a novelty until just a couple of years back. Presently in almost any nation on the planet, you can locate an astounding scope of mobile food sellers offering practically any sort of food from burgers to nachos to ribs. Consistently, the number and diversity of trucks and food on offer develops.

My personal top choice style of food trucks is the Tex-Mex based food trucks. Nachos, gourmet nacho cheddar, tacos, and burritos are on the finest food I've ever had. There is something in particular about a warm and naturally made foil-wrapped burrito that just gives me that warm and fluffy feeling!

At that point there's the nachos, once I've had only a taste of that gooey liquefied nacho cheddar sauce and some fresh homemade stew, I basically can't get enough. Something so simple can taste so delicious. Not only is the flavor of these foods so divine, yet the costs are top-notch. Setting off to a standard eatery for a similar food will usually cost double.

The food truck culture has developed into such a major industry, that individuals really make a living from simply running their own truck. It is not a hobby-based business anymore. There are even sites committed to showing you precisely where a specific food truck is on some random day specifically urban areas. The Australian site 'Where The Truck At' appears more than 100 food trucks across 7 urban areas and gives you a guide and time with respect to when the food trucks will be serving.

Across practically any nation, there are endless mobile food van catalogs offering the same information. I'm not surprised about why either. With such an interest in this style of cooking, there is a need to guide and track the areas for the many buyers every day who anticipate their food truck lunch.

The incredible thing about all these various foods being acquainted with individuals on the streets is that individuals are currently turning out to be increasingly adventurous when cooking at home. For instance, you may have a genuine craving for a real burrito, however, perhaps the food vans have all shut for the afternoon. In this way, you do the following best thing, you make it yourself!

Fortunately sourcing the ingredients isn't as hard as it used to be either, in certainty you can discover most items on the web and have them conveyed. In practically any nation now you can arrange specific ingredients and have them sent to your doorstep. In North and South America and across Europe it's very easy to discover specialist items.

In other nations, it tends to be progressively difficult. Across Asia Pacific, for instance, a few countries have a lot smaller populace and are less affected by the food truck culture which implies there is constrained assortment on offer. Fortunately for anybody wanting the genuine nacho cheese, American sauces or Mexican chilies you can get them online from a couple of dedicated sites.

The most concerning issue with the food truck industry is choosing what to have for lunch every day!

Chapter 14: FOOD TRUCKS - AN IDEAL ALTERNATIVE TO RESTAURANTS

The whole of America is enjoying the new hype of food trucks that arrives at wherever you are. Individuals are simply taking the delight of this new contort where healthy value is given more significance. These can likewise be considered as mobile eateries that can be spotted anywhere. By looking at the environmentally safe aspect, food trucks ends up being a superior alternative than the cafés by saving space, energy, and time.

When restaurants are incredibly built on blocks and are immobile, the food trucks end up being a superior choice as it can move to numerous spots. Infrastructure maintenance is insignificant when contrasted with that of cafés. The last consumes a physical space day and night where as the previous coexists with a curb-side spot during the working hours and is then taken to the parking area later on.

The vitality utilization must be thought about as the food truck requires truly less lights and other necessities where as you need to spend a great deal with regards to a café/restaurant. This new idea laid forward is all the more promising and acknowledged by the greater part as it is truly unique and new.

When the expenses are cut down enormously, what results is good food at low costs that is moderate for everybody. In the present fast paced world and expansion striking high, individuals are after some superb approaches to appreciate with least sum spent. This is the primary reason behind why the dominant part gives more significance to such recently presented techniques for serving great and crisp food.

Food trucks are without a doubt viewed as a better decision upon eateries because of a few components referencedabove. In any case, it contrasts from person to person as individuals have their own top picks and genuine opinions. There are obviously a few favorable circumstances of eateries over the food trucks that ought to be considered and it relies upon the individuals to settle on their decision.

The new gourmet trucks are doing their most extreme to extend broadly and move to other parts of the world. Food gatherings are constantly a total package for satisfaction and entertainemnt. These new developing organizations are concentrating via social media to bring individuals near their locations. The community that they develop makes certain to follow with prominence and rising spots. Tomorrow's fate is obscure and food trucks are making a transformation that will sooner be consumed by the individuals all over the globe.

What Is A Food Truck And The Reasons Behind Its Popularity

A food truck otherwise called a 'mobile kitchen' or a 'café on wheels' is a famous catering idea all through the world and has been being used since many years. Food joints where individuals can stop by for a speedy bite are found in plenty, particularly in places like parkways, outside workplaces, parks, festivals and well known markets and this makes the entire idea of an eatery on wheels much all the more alluring. The restaurant proprietor can do significantly more business than a conventional eatery by providing food at various venues around the same time. Likewise, due to less overhead costs, they require lesser business venture.

Since time immemorial, individuals have constantly longed for good food, something which is like an enthusiasm both for individuals who love to eat and the individuals who love to cook. What's more, appropriately, there is no deficiency of cafés serving various cooking styles at various budget all over. However, food trucks offer a totally extraordinary experience and this is the thing that makes them so uncommon. A food truck is a versatile setting or a vehicle that serves food on the go.

These portable cafés have numerous points of interest over customary eateries - initially, they can go to where the clients are instead of the clients making a trip to reach a specific eatery. As they are eatery on wheels, they can serve food to an assortment of areas within a single day, accordingly expanding their deals and going to regions where there are loads of individuals like fairs, occasions, and so on. Furthermore, the overhead costs of a café on wheels are significantly less than a standard eatery as they require lesser staff and very little infrastructure either.

Another significant benefit of a food truck for the proprietor is that a great deal of business can be generated each and every day, with only a little careful arranging as opposed to hanging tight for clients, a mobile kitchen can go to places where there are clients. For example, it can cater to office-goers in the morning and night, work together outside schools or universities toward the evening and serve clients outside shopping centers and malls in the late night.

However, what makes food trucks or café on wheels enticing to clients is significantly all the more fascinating. Individuals are consistently watchful for new and intriguing ideas particularly in food and a café that moves has consistently gotten their extravagant. The assortment of dishes served at spending neighborly costs, additionally makes mobile eateries mainstream and individuals generally throng them for testing delicious food at moderate costs. Likewise, the whole procedure of requesting food is quicker, as clients don't have to hang tight for a table, they can just request and eat on the go. Additionally, gone are the days, when a food truck was related to a gray van serving food for the lower classes.

Nowadays, numerous 5-star gourmet specialists, successful restaurateurs and idiosyncratic foodies are all finding the marvels of a food truck, while getting a large group of new highlights of style and present-day amenities. Thus, why not make a beeline for a close-by restaurant and test the lip-smacking cuisine they serve for your own, to find what makes these mobile eateries so mainstream.

WEDDING MENU TREND - FOOD TRUCKS

At this point, many people are most likely acquainted with the solace food pattern that has been so well known for wedding receptions in recent years. This desire for recognizable and unassuming fare has been taken to the following level with one of the most current wedding trends. The coolest wedding receptions nowadays highlight food trucks as a feature of the menu.

You may think about how a food truck can be incorporated into an elegant wedding. The appropriate response is that it is in reality pretty easy, as long as the reception will happen outside. On numerous occasions, the food truck is, in addition, a more standard presentation of food. It could be an extraordinary component for the cocktail hour, some portion of the principle supper time, or a late-night surprise. It isn't too difficult to even consider finding a food truck to go to your wedding since the vast majority of them work during the day, and most wedding receptions happen later at night. It is generally a matter of organizing your preferred road merchant with your wedding reception venue coordinator.

Food truck fare is uncomplicated by definition. Couples usually simply pick whatever they love the best. It may be a sausage truck, one serving burritos, an ice cream truck or a pizza van (so a good time for a summer wedding!). If you don't have space for a whole truck at your reception, you can employ a merchant with a push truck. That is likewise an incredible alternative for bringing this idea inside. You could have a cotton treat truck, a new popcorn man, or whatever makes you excited.

Consider what you like to eat on the street. Perhaps it's cheeseburgers or dumplings or even little crepes. If it very well may be served from a truck or cart, it very well may be an incredible choice for a fun reception surprise. This is a particularly flawless approach to acquaint your loved ones with your local favorites. Remember your school days by inviting the same truck that you used to visit while in transit to class or on game day. Or then again acquaint your family with another flavor that is mainstream where you live now, for example, Cuban food if you recently migrated to

Miami. When served alongside increasingly run of the mill menu choices, the food truck or truck can enable you to spice things up a bit, while still offering things you realize everybody will like.

You'll need to ensure you get loads of images of guests enjoying the food truck at your reception. Such an essential part of your wedding will make for awesome and special photographs. Simply think about the fun images you'll get of the mother of the bride in her exquisite dress and pearl necklace snacking on a new funnel cake from a truck or a cut of pizza! If you intend to serve something extremely muddled like chili dogs, the bride may want to have something she can toss on to shield her outfit from spills. One bride, I knew glanced fantastic in her handcrafted outfit and unique pearl neckband - until she got a major sprinkle of mustard from hot dog down the front of her wedding dress. The bride should definitely get to enjoy the delectable truck food; take care not to let it ruin your outfit.

So now you know: if you need to surprise your guests, procure a food truck to cater part of your wedding reception. It is a fun pattern that can be adjusted to suit practically any wedding, and your guests will absolutely see the food truck as a delicious and memorable part of your wedding!

HOW TO SELL OUT YOUR ENTIRE FOOD TRUCK IN 45 MINUTES

Everyone adores food trucks. Whenever a new one springs up on the corner there is constantly a buzz and excitement all around. But the fact of the matter is getting traffic to your truck isn't as simple as it sounds right off the bat. Obviously, the main guideline is location, but there are a couple of key strategies you can use to give yourself a lift - regardless of where your truck is situated.

Food Trucks are an incredible resource for any café brand. Not only would they be enormously profitable, but they also work superbly of getting out in the streets and making your brand known. They offer exposure to your eatery and your brand in new places - making more clients and boosting your deals.

But how would you get more individuals to go to your food truck? Clearly, location is basic. Finding the right corner or cross street will have a tremendous effect on the success of your food truck. There is another technique that can have an enormous impact on the success of any food truck.

Location-based services offer an extraordinary device for promoting and advertising food trucks. Consider - what better approach to generate buzz and get individuals to your truck than to offer them an incentive for making a trip and checking in. Ice cream truck? Give them a free additional scoop. Get individuals excited and involved. Here are a couple techniques for generating enough buzz to sell out your food truck in less than 60 minutes!

Have a free giveaway at your truck. Try do giveaways, a free T-Shirt or something fun and seasonal.

Tell people to check-in at a particular time. Generate a major crowd and a lot of buzz, have individuals check in simultaneously.

Use Foursquare "Swarm" Badge as an impetus to get everybody to check in at once.

Host your location-based occasion on during a special day - during a vacation or end of the week when more individuals are all over the place.

Have your check-in special be a "group discount" - like Groupon - where you check-in with a group of four and get a free giveaway - this urges more individuals to come visit your food truck and people will bring their friends.

Most importantly - have a lot of fun - location-based software is an incredible method to create buzz and advance your mobile food stand, but it's also an interesting way to generate new deals. Appreciate it and learn how else you can utilize location-based service to help fabricate your sales.

Food trucks are an extraordinary opportunity for any restaurant - and location-based advertising provides a new and exciting way to generate traffic and buzz for your food truck.

Chapter 15: ADJUSTING YOUR FOOD TRUCK'S MENU TO ENTICE MORE CUSTOMERS

Your menu is in excess of a listing board for the entirety of your catering truck's dishes, sides, and treats. It's the primary thing your clients' eyes take a look at after they smell what's cooking and read your truck's name from its outside. You have their attention, yet will you hold it?

Your menu, besides your food trailer's exterior structure, is your greatest commercial. By utilizing various fonts, colors, pictures, sizes, your menu will help figure out what your clients purchase - that is, if they purchase from your mobile food remain rather than the one down the road. Every individual will take a look at your menu board to choose if your truck has preferred alternatives over other ones the person in question has passed already and will pass later.

However, a lot of your clients' choices will be based on how the menu shows up - practically the same amount as the clients will base their choices with respect to the food that is on the menu. Here are a couple of approaches to make your menu more appealing to clients and also ways to expand normal spend per client at your catering truck:

- Distance your menu from the customary section design. Not only is the section design boring, however, it additionally will, in general, make clients analyze the costs of each dish when they're all lined up over each another. in order to battle this, utilize the space on your food truck's menu to make intriguing areas that hold each individually course (appetizers, desserts, mains), but one in which each dish in a similar classification is someway isolated from other dishes -, for example, with a line, box, or diverse hued marker/textual style.

- Don't utilize $$$. We see eateries grabbing hold of this $ - less trend the entirety of the nation. It originally started at more costly cafés and afterward advanced down to customary and mobile diners. Psychologists have discovered that menus without dollar signs enable the client to concentrate on the real wording on the menu, as opposed to on the cost. Clients wind up associating the number going with the meal's description with how great the dinner will be rather than how much the feast will cost. By wiping out dollar signs from your menu, your menu turns into a rundown of dinners and not a rundown of costs.

- Be expressive. Most clients fully trust the menu. This implies extra information on the menu item if this information isn't recorded or at least indicated by the menu board itself. Particularly with more noteworthy accentuation on where food begins or what it's quality/image is these days, it's beneficial to list descriptive labels underneath your menu items - particularly if your food truck is charging premiums on items that give off an impression of being average, for example, a burger or Philly cheesesteak.

- Be attentive to prime real estate on your food truck's menu board. Your client's eyes will initially hit the upper right-hand corner of the menu board and afterward, they'll go directly to the whole left half of the board. Ensure these regions have something particularly luring for the client's eyes (and hopefully mouths) to feast on.

HOW SHOULD YOU DESIGN YOUR FOOD TRUCK'S MENU BOARD?

In some ways, your menu board ought to be similarly appealing to your client as when the client sees the genuine meals that your food trailer gets ready. No - this doesn't imply that you ought to have pictures of your food on your menu board, in essence. Rather, your menu ought to be visually appealing. Close your eyes and picture the menu at your preferred eatery - or even cheap food joint, for this issue. Is the menu basic, striking, or brilliant? How is the content designed? A bigger number of chances than not, the menu at your preferred spot is stylishly satisfying in one form or another.

So what does having a decent menu have to do with your catering truck? Everything. Your menu offers credibility to your food things - particularly when another client stops at your mobile food stand. If your menu board is befuddling, boring or outright appalling you'll lose walk-ups before you get an opportunity to convert them into clients.

Keep in mind, your menu board is a message from you to your clients. Its main responsibility is to sell your meals. To utilize this tool adequately, the board must communicate the appropriate messages and lead your guests to the higher-benefit items.

All in all, in what capacity would it be a good idea for you to structure the menu board for your food truck?

To begin with, take the subject and idea of your truck into thought. Is there a particular textual style and color scheme that you use to design your food trailer? Assuming this is the case, you might need to utilize these on your menu board. In any case, if the textual styles are difficult to read in smaller print, consider utilizing progressively decipherable textual style types, for example, "Times New Roman" or "Arial." The same guideline applies to color; guarantee that the shading is effectively discernible on the menu board background color.

When designing your board, you ought to likewise cautiously plan the format of your menu. Side items, fundamental things, and sweets ought to be assembled likewise in titled areas, just as they are on café menus. The description of everything should take up close to two lines underneath each title. The depiction region is an opportunity for you to describe and sell the product to the client. It ought to be enticing and simple. Nobody needs to read a novel when the person in question is requesting a feast - particularly from a mobile food stand.

In addition, your menu board, you might need to make printed materials to pass out to your clients when they visit the stand. These sorts of materials fill in as publicizing promotions also, since the client may show the menu to companions or hang it up at work. You can likewise offer a catering menu - if you might want to open up this opportunity for your mobile food stand.

You'll be astonished at what number of clients approach you to inquire as to whether you cater.

Here's my supposition: Ask an expert graphic designer for help with your menu. It might appear to be a basic errand that you need to finish without anyone else, and I get that. But, this is a chart that all of your clients are going to see regularly. What's more, if you make printed materials to oblige it, this menu will get considerably more exposure. It's important that your food truck brand is constantly represented in a positive light, particularly when your tasty food items aren't there to back it up.

Chapter 16: EASY STEPS TO BUILD A GREAT FOOD TRUCK

The ascent in the predominance of food trucks has been an incredible trend to observe.

People line up outside of a fixed vehicle holding on for a debased dish of Korean BBQ or light, flaky cake or a decent succulent burger. It's not high-end food, but it is eating without the costly and luxurious appeal of cafés. Fr the past few years, the idea of inexpensive food has changed a ton. A couple of decades back, individuals legitimately abstained from eating from the street stalls on the grounds that, in most cases, the items were unhygienic. However, nowadays, new and energizing trucks are being opened that are serving new and sound dishes. Much the same as eateries, the dish is prepared immediately and served hot.

Setting up the tight vehicle is important

Sure individuals who love your dishes will constantly return to have some more, but in the case of new clients, they will choose if they need to move toward your food truck or not relying upon the appearance of the vehicle. You can serve some lip-smacking dishes, but if your vehicle is uninteresting and dull, nobody will come to purchase your dishes.

It is not a foregone conclusion that you generally need to utilize proficient fashioners and temporary workers to create a truck for you. In the event that you are certain about yourself, you can do it all alone. These simple steps should assist you in building the best vehicle for your mobile café.

Determine the kind of equipment

In step one, you will choose the kind of truck you need, alongside the rigging expected to serve the sustenance. Taking everything into account, if you pick a coffee truck, you will have altogether extraordinary space and equipment essentials than a burger van.

Get a piece of paper or open a Word archive and begin to record all of the gear you need to include on your future truck. This could incorporate a fridge, cooler, profound frier, flame torches, and storage room to list several the fundamentals.

Step 1: Find a vehicle

After you have decided the design, it's time to really take a few to get a hold of a vehicle that really takes into account your necessities. Few organizations offer these sorts of mobile diner units at exceptionally competitive costs. You ought to get a statement from these organizations to discover where you stand.

Step 2: Clean and mark out the area

After you have obtained the vehicle, it's time to clean it. From that point onward, it's time to mark out the areas where you need to place your cooking equipment. You ought to choose where you need to place your fridge, oven, washbowls, coolers, fryers, and shelves.

Step 3: Set up the wiring

The essential thought behind these mobile cafés is that they will require electrical wiring that runs on batteries. Set up the entire establishment before installing the equipment.

Step 4: Decorate the interiors

It's imperative to structure your truck in a manner which will attract others. The structures, both inside and outside should be appealing and energetic.

Step 5: Cut counters and install ACs

Cut a counter in the vehicle on one side from where you will be passing your dishes to the clients. This opening ought to be sufficiently large to accommodate huge crowds.

Lunch Truck - Are You Right For A Lunch Truck Business?

The Lunch Truck/Food Truck industry is booming at this moment; I surf the net constantly and converse with a lot of proprietors, administrators, workers and helpers in the food business, they all reveal to me something very similar.

Individuals go crazy spending cash, their well-deserved cash, on lunch trucks- - purchasing or renting, making crazy deals in the purchasing a lunch truck business.

The reality of the situation is that people have a consuming sensation to spend, all their cash, believing this is the path to the promised land, such as putting down $10,000. and taking care of the credit and discovering several months after the fact that this business isn't for them and selling a large portion of the value you have purchased the lunch truck business for.

The odds are stacked against you, it isn't so much that you can't deal with that installment. The reality of the situation, It's on the grounds that you're not trained in the right training in setting up your new venture with your business.

Individuals simply jump directly into the pit of purchasing a lunch truck,

The standards of Louie just let me know, I have the video:

1. Work with a lunch truck proprietor so you can train and experience the mechanics of learning the ropes for two seasons.
2. You can lease a route, most grocery store has truck courses that is entrenched with route that you can work with for quite a while and the hook is that you need to purchase the items from the supermarket, most supermarket charges $100.00 to $150.00 per day for the route and they deal with a large portion

of the things, your responsible for gas, wear and tear.

3   You can get proprietor financing after you become familiar with the ropes, don't hop into and business that you're going to regret.

Chapter 17: HOW THE TRUCKING INDUSTRY IS ADAPTING TO THE SUSTAINABLE FOOD TREND

The trucking business has had an unpleasant couple of years. From load deficiencies and rising fuel expenses to lost jobs and stricter guidelines, the trucking business has been a bleak scene. In any case, with employments expanding again and business picking, things have started to look up for truckers and trucking organizations. Be that as it may, with new business comes new difficulties and the truth will surface eventually how well the trucking business adjusts to the new food patterns, more particularly, the sustainable food pattern.

A recently discharged article by the Journal of Commerce examines how the interest from food makers and retailers for a sustainable and green food supply chain is influencing the trucking business. With the green pattern by food retailers and producers gaining steam, the trucking business is seeing more freight being delivered in less loads. For the trucking business that implies that the customary semi-trailer shipping has diminished while shipping techniques, for example, trains and barges are being used more frequently.

Organizations such as Kraft, as referred to by the Journal of Commerce article, have cut in excess of 50 million trucking miles in the last 4 years - and that is just one organization. Numerous other organizations have emulated Kraft's footsteps in looking for progressively manageable transportation techniques for their items. Kraft specifically, however, has even ventured to such an extreme as to patch up their truck fleets in addition to utilizing diverse delivery strategies. Kraft's truck fleets have been retrofitted as diesel-electric hybrids and they each have RouteMax refrigerated truck bodies.

In what appears to be an odd move by food ventures, 85 percent of the expanded or kept up their sustainable activities during the recession. Although sustainable practices will in general cost more, the food business decided to build their spending on sustainable activities because of purchaser demand. Despite the fact that much of the expense of sustainable practices is given to the customer, the food business has not hindered their green endeavors.

Although the volume of shipments for refrigerated trucks has diminished somewhere in the range of 3-15% over the previous year, shippers are trying to expand their number of pallets per shipment so as to decrease carbon emanations and generally trucking miles. The expansion in pallets per shipment has been a genuinely easy assignment for trucking organizations on the grounds that the food business has reduced excessive packaging.

By and large, the trucking business has a ton of work to do so as to adjust to the changing needs of the food business, for example, retrofitting their current trucks and remarketing themselves to food organizations as green complaints. In any case, it seems like the economical food pattern will continue, hence if trucking organizations need to remain focused on different types of sustainable transportation, they should start transitioning their trucks and their business models.

FOOD SERVICES ON A VEHICLE

The business of food service provision in a distant territory is called Catering. Catering might be in various structures given that there is the essence of serving food to clients. One fascinating kind of catering is Mobile Catering where food is sold and served from inside a vehicle or car. It is likewise realized that in certain nations, Mobile catering is a piece of their urban culture.

Various sorts of vehicles are utilized in providing Mobile Catering to purchasers:

- A Street Cart is a trailer without engine or motor to help in the deal and promoting of street foods to nearby pedestrian for its regular areas are in walkway or parks. This truck is towed and pulled to the selling area either by a car, a motorcycle or basically by hand. It is a mobile kitchen that is regularly worked with onboard warming and refrigeration includes so as to cook foods instantly. A sausage or hotdog stand is one case of a road truck catering service. Different foods sold in road trucks are bagels, coffee, doughnuts, sandwiches, burritos and tacos. Some street trucks are subsidiary with eateries, therefore the foods served in the truck are the equivalent of the foods served in the eatery.

- A Catering Truck is comparative with that of a Street Cart in terms of service provided. The distinctions are that the previous conveys enormous volumes of food (as in a frozen yogurt van) to be served and offered to clients and could be driven independently. There are two striking kinds of Catering Trucks: * A Mobile Food Preparation Vehicle (MFPV) is typically set up with a driver and a cook. In this catering truck, foods are cooked and arranged as clients request, along these lines provisions which can be prepared easily are like various sorts of sandwiches are served. * An Industrial Catering Vehicle (ICV) is a catering truck that sells pre-packaged foods. A driver and an individual to help the clients are the standard staff in an ICV.

- A Food Truck is a mobile venue that sells food. There are some which ell solidified or prepackaged foods, others serve an assortment of foodstuffs and named as 'eatery on-wheels, while others serve specific meals like breakfast, lunch or snacks. There is an adaptability in the menu since foods can be set up as you order or can be requested in advance. Food trucks are known to cater to occasions like festivals, construction sites or games where potential purchasers require ordinary meal chows.
- A Concession Trailer is fabricated like a mobile kitchen with prepared to utilize cooking and capacity highlights, but can't be moved or driven without anyone else. Subsequently, concession trailers are frequently situated in enduring occasions, for example, mobile carnivals or funfairs or local feasts.

- Mobile catering vehicles are not just confined or restricted to be utilized in profit earning exercises or by individuals who need to earn from cooking. A few vehicles are utilized to give food to residents of spots influenced by natural events and whose infrastructures are harmed also.

STARTING YOUR OWN MOBILE FOOD CART

Have you seen a food truck while you were strolling through town recently? Possibly you were strolling through a festival or perhaps you were simply strolling down the road when you saw it. Well without a doubt, somehow, you have seen at least one (most likely many) however, have you at any point pondered owning one for yourself? Sure you've most likely eaten at one preceding. Possibly you've had sausages or frozen yogurt. You may have even had something like tacos or soup. The reality is that there is a wide range of various kinds of food that you can get from one of these awesome mobile kitchens. What's more, the range is developing constantly.

In case you're thinking, 'For what reason would I need to own one?' Well, the response to that might be a lot less difficult than you think. How regularly do you think you stop and eat at a food truck? Do you stop for unique events or do you eat at one often? Well, in all honesty, one of these is reason to begin a food truck business of your own. If you just eat there on special occasions, then that implies you consider eating at a food truck as being something exceptional. Well so do others. If you eat there habitually, then you realize that others are doing likewise. The truth of the matter is, food trucks flourish and the people who eat at them are fans - this is a flourishing and developing industry.

Why Get a Food Cart?

Food trucks can be incredible investments since they are providing an item and service that is a consumable - so regardless of whether somebody purchased from you yesterday, that doesn't imply that is the end of their custom. Unlike other services and products that you may just need once, or occasionally, or every other day or week, even, individuals need to eat routinely! With a bustling way of life that we all lead nowadays, more individuals are eating out and not preparing their own food so much any longer. So cashflow in from happy clients can be useful for those running an incredible food truck.

When you initially get a truck you're going to need the truck itself and the food to make in it. Then you simply need to get yourself a spot to set up and trust that the individuals will start appearing. You'll be able to make money the first day unlike most other organizations since food isn't an extravagance, it's a necessity. It's somewhat more complicated than that, however you get the idea.

Food trucks are starting to develop in notoriety as an ever-increasing number of individuals understand the advantages of starting one for themselves. You can make almost any food conceivable and you'll get every single distinctive kind of individuals to come and check it out. As long as you set up for business normally, give a product and service that individuals need, run your food truck as a business and toss personality and enthusiasm into it, you'll be on track to make a decent benefit and you'll be able to meet a wide range of new individuals simultaneously and give them an eating experience to always remember. Who wouldn't care to make their living that way?

Who Stops at Food Carts?

For the individuals eating at these trucks, they never appear to grow old either. That is on the grounds that individuals truly appreciate getting those uncommon foods at the festival (like pan-fried doughnuts or cinnamon almonds). These are extraordinary treats that the old and youthful alike can't leave behind when they arrive at a festival. Then you have the food trucks that are perched on typical streets, the ones that offer normal foods to grown-ups searching for a snappy lunch on their way back to work. These trucks are extraordinary too on the grounds that the food they offer is reasonable and quick. Numerous business people stop at food trucks each day and more seem to pick this lunch choice constantly.

If you need to fire up your own business, however, aren't sure what to get into then look at these mobile kitchens. If you've always longed for having your own café but are frightened by the cost and duty required, then food trucks can regularly be a venturing stone as they get you into the foodservice industry for a lower investment and you can build your name and notoriety your product - then the progression to a full-blown store-front eatery can be simpler. Food trucks are moderately simple to begin and they're famous for new entrepreneurs as well as for the overall population too. Numerous food truck proprietors love running it and love that everybody around affection coming to them for some extraordinary quality food at reasonable costs and quick service. It's win-win for everybody involved. But in case you're as yet not persuaded there's still more to this story.

Food trucks are extraordinary. For individuals who live in large urban areas they may turn out to be simply one more part of the landscape (even if that doesn't prevent them from eating at them often) but for individuals who aren't accustomed to the enormous city, the idea of stopping at a food truck is fascinating, new and unique. These individuals couldn't care less that the food you're serving isn't really gourmet (although you'll be flabbergasted at the assortment of food types accessible from mobile food sellers nowadays), all they need is to give it a shot since that is the thing that 'enormous city individuals' do. So there's consistently another person ready to try what you bring to the table.

The Freedom to Move

Another incredible thing about food trucks as a business is that they can be on the move. If you pick a spot and it ends up being dead space where nobody goes then you're stuck with it. A food truck gives you the opportunity to move around and go anywhere you want. So if one day you're on a street corner that simply doesn't have a lot of business, the following day you can move elsewhere. If you begin on one street but it begins to get exhausting you can move along from that point also. You can even be a mobile street truck that moves around throughout the day.

Getting started is simple with the right knowledge, making profit is totally feasible if you've set yourself upright, and you never need to stress over coming up short on individuals to serve or getting bored with the view. Since there's less risk in a mobile food seller business than numerous other kinds of private ventures, you and your new food truck can be off to an extraordinary beginning right from the beginning.

Reasons to Purchase a Mobile Food Concession Business

The concession business is becoming a well-known approach to make a living in the restaurant business. There are a few reasons to go into this sort of business before you attempt to begin a stationary café. To begin with, starting a mobile concession business is a lot smaller venture to make. Second, you can build up a name in the neighborhood community. Finally, since the organization will be transportable, you can attempt various kinds of locations before settling on only one. Subsequent to opening your very own food concession business, you may decide to keep it forever, start a café/ restaurant in addition to it, or progress easily into the eating establishment you always longed for.

The principal reason to decide to run a mobile food concession business before a bricks and mortar café is that it is a lot smaller financial burden and risk to take upon your shoulders. If you are new to the food business, there is more risk in buying a stationary business than if you have past industry experience. If running a café is something you constantly needed to do, this is an extraordinary method to begin little and to stir your way up to the position you want. This sort of business is little and a lot simpler to contain and to run than simply hopping into a 75 seat restaurant. A concession trailer or food truck can be in a huge number of dollars to invest while a conventional eating establishment can get into the thousands of dollars and that's just the beginning. Along these lines, being practical, if your business fails, you will have invested less cash.

Another reason to sell food from a concession trailer initially is that you can go ahead and build up an organization named in the local community. If you don't have the resources immediately to put into an eatery, the concession trailer can be the methods by which you get those resources. At the same time, you are developing benefit and offering to local people, you are getting your name and story out to the individuals. If your customary clients pass another eatery with a similar name as your concession business, you will be able to attract in repeat clients while never having opened the conventional restaurant.

Finally, another reason to start up a food concession trailer or a food truck is that since the organization is transportable, you can move to another area if the one you are in isn't fruitful. In many cases with customary cafés, you get into an area that, out of the blue, there is simply not good business. You may have all the components a decent diner needs: a great neighborhood, a lot of traffic activity, and incredible food and service, despite everything it doesn't earn the salary you expect. Unfortunately, with a stationary eatery, there isn't a lot of you can do except stick it out or surrender. In any case, one of the particular favorable circumstances of a mobile truck or trailer is that you can move where the cash is; you simply need to locate that ideal spot.

Owning a café is a fantasy for some individuals, however, it isn't constantly open. A lot simpler, less expensive, and more convenient approach to consider going all in the business is to begin your very own food concession business. These and other reasons give evidence that beginning the smaller investment of a concession trailer can be an exceptionally brilliant idea.

There are few reasons to pick a mobile food business over a customary stationary café. It is a less expensive investment, you can set up a name for yourself, and you can likewise move your business to another area if it isn't profiting as expected

Chapter 18: CONCLUSION

Lunch trucks have been in use for over 2 decades. The fundamental thought of the lunch truck is to serve food to individuals situated in various areas. The main lunch truck was invented way back in the nineteenth-century for the military which served food to their officers. This was known as mobile lunch service. They were served with coffee and snacks which were easy to make with the technology they had during their time. Presently, as technology has progressed and given us various equipments to kitchen use, the advanced lunch trucks carry all the vital and current amenities that are required in the kitchen.

Lunch trucks are known for their benefits. When contrasted and the stationary cafés, lunch trucks have indicated great profit and furthermore great client base.

If you can give the clients great quality of food that they can afford, you can likewise expect few loyal client following in various areas that you intend to go around. As you would be moving from one spot to others, you have the chance to serve more individuals and with various menu choices.

The underlying investment that you would make is on the vehicle. With numerous models accessible in the market, you should pick the one which will fill your need. The following stage in the investment would be the equipment that you require, for example, the stainless steel sinks, oven, fridge, and other embellishments, for example, the cutlery sets, plates and so forth before you start off with your new business, there are scarcely any rules that you need to follow. With the government presenting stringent guidelines for mobile food services, it is fundamental for you to keep every one of the principles so as to remain in the business.

You are likewise required to get the mobile food service permit from the legislature before you kick-off of your business. You can go to the local government authorities who will help you with respect to the license details. The modern lunch trucks are furnished with current sterile solutions to keeping the environment and the earth clean giving a hygienic atmosphere for the clients to eat their food.

If you can't invest in the underlying amount that is required for obtaining the vehicle and also the important embellishments for the kitchen, you can then approach a franchise from where you can purchase his food items. When you secure a deal with a franchise, they will give all of you the important equipment for the kitchen and furthermore the lunch truck. The main thing that you have to do is to head to various areas and serve the food. Regardless of the path you pick, mobile food service permit is a must.

If you might want to expand the benefits to the following level, present additional services which will satisfy the clients and furthermore at the same time increases the client base as well as the loyal customer following. Aside from the lunch boxes that you provide, you can likewise present ice creams and desserts in the menu.

CPSIA information can be obtained
at www.ICGtesting.com
Printed in the USA
LVHW080404250521
688340LV00002B/331

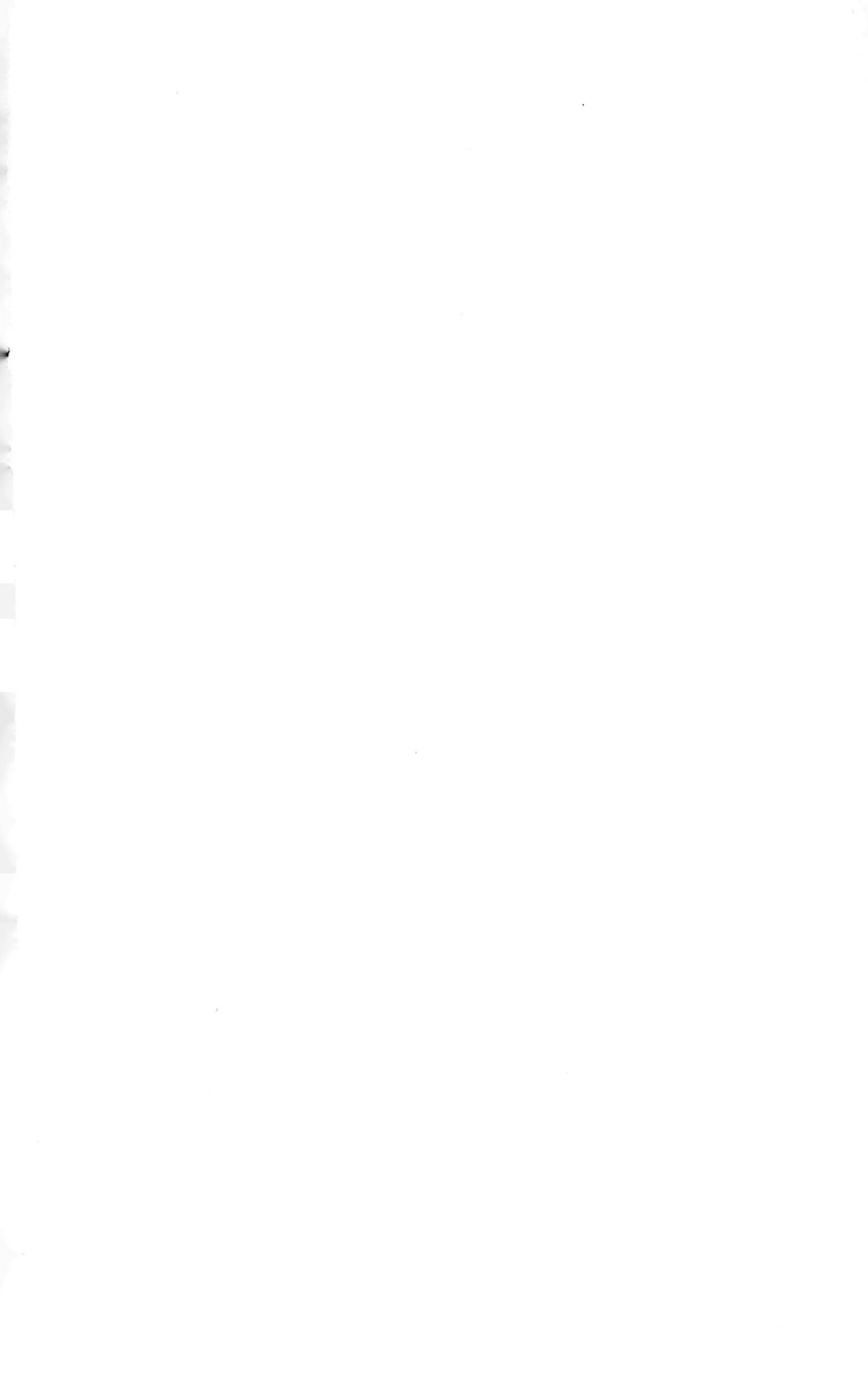